LIVING LOVED

LIVING LOVED

A PATH TO PEACE

Marie
You are loved!
Marie Maguire

Marie Maguire

For permission requests, write to the author addressed:
"Attention: Permissions" at LivingLoved@Marie-Maguire.com
Printed in the United States of America
First Printing, 2017
ISBN-13: 9781542463164
ISBN-10: 1542463165
www.Marie-Maguire.com
Cover designed by the author
Cover image by iStock Photo – used with permission
Author image by Julie Calvez Stinson – used with permission

Dedication

To all of my teachers along the way, this book is the fruit of our labors.

GRATITUDE

Dear Beautiful Souls,

I am thankful for all the good, easy and fun times I've had and the wonderful people I've met, of course. Yet I am especially thankful for every difficult, challenging, scary, and sad moment (and person) that has entered my life. These include, and are not limited to, sexual abuse, verbal violence, rejection, and grief. You may shake your head and even wonder if I've lost my marbles. I'm thankful for the challenging times and people because they were the perfect setup for growing. The tough times roused me from my deafness, opened my awareness, and caused me to cry out for understanding and mercy, thus creating an authentic connection to myself and to God. In other words: the tough times woke me up! The waking up moved me down the path through fear to living loved.

From a ground-level perspective, it couldn't have been easy for anyone else who participated in my own personal journey from fear to love. (I apologize!) Along the way there were many confused actions as I gathered experience and gained wisdom. I have grown so far, so fast, with many twists and turns. My life was tough for me to handle until I grasped the higher purpose behind it all. This book will shed light on that purpose.

From a higher point of view, I believe each of us chose to live this life together, even if we don't remember, or currently appreciate, the arrangement. It comforts me to think that we agreed, before entering this lifetime, to help each other learn whatever lessons we desired for our continued growth. Each circumstance, each relationship, and each challenge has been what was needed to help us grow, and these have provided an opportunity to heal any separation within ourselves and with God (Love Itself).

I am thankful for each of you my dear family, friends, clients, neighbors, and "enemies" for teaching me what I needed to know. Thank you for sharing this life with me. Come, let us continue to wake up and love ourselves, and one another, with a love that is timeless.

~ Marie Maguire

FORWARD

I'VE KNOWN MARIE Maguire for over twenty years and it's no exaggeration to say that her friendship has been one of the great gifts of my life. Almost every time we're together, we talk about the miracle of finding each other in this lifetime. When we first met I was living with blinders on and hiding a deep sense of fear so well that no one knew, except Marie. I felt pretty confident that I had life all figured out. Why ask questions when you have all the answers? I needed this belief to feel like I was in control.

I was a rule follower. I held firmly to my religious standards and never rocked the boat. Then I met Marie. The first thing I noticed about my new friend was that she seemed different than the other Christians I knew. She seemed cracked or broken, in the best sense of the word, and that intrigued me and conversely left me feeling very unsettled. The mystic in me had met another mystic, and my soul recognized it right away. It wasn't exactly comfortable being around her because she could see that I was hiding, and I didn't like being seen. More than anything, I wanted to come out of hiding and intuitively knew that she could help.

When we met, unbeknownst to me, she had already been surviving a nearly ten-year-long journey into the dark night of the soul. Though Marie didn't use the term, it was a time of deep inner transformation similar to what the caterpillar goes through in the cocoon; darkness, unknowing, and dissolving. It wasn't until I stumbled into my own dark night two years later that I began to crack and break open. That was the very thing that made Marie so different and intriguing to me. My journey began taking me into deep uncharted waters where my boat was not only rocking; it had been turned inside out!

A lifetime of playing by the rules, trying to be nice and not asking questions, had forced me into a very narrow, shadowy corner. I felt trapped in the middle of a spiritual crisis as I tried to keep my worldview from shifting, to keep my world from changing. The irony is that we aren't actually designed to stay comfortable and fulfilled within small belief systems. My ideas were not bad or wrong. I was simply outgrowing the self-imposed container that was holding those ideas and beliefs so that I could become my authentic self. I was the caterpillar outgrowing his earth-bound body to become air bound. We are destined to fly!

Marie was thrilled to see me break open because she is one who understands such things. In fact, in the middle of my first breakdown, she smiled and said, "I'm so excited!" At other times when I thought I was losing my mind, she would say, "Put one foot in front of the other. You don't have to do anything, or be anything different, take only actions inspired by love."

It wasn't only what she said that brought me safely through, it was the rock steady, deeply compassionate, motherly knowing in her soul, and in her eyes, in which I completely trusted.

Though Marie was further along on the journey of transformation, we encouraged each other to run wild toward more and more freedom. And magic! Together, our worldviews began changing at an incredibly fast rate, often leaving us both feeling lost and unhinged. We would check in with each other to make sure we weren't lost and to get some reassurance that God still loved us. We asked big questions and explored new vistas, and that makes even the strongest of souls feel disoriented. A little at a time, we ventured out into the unknown, studied other faiths or metaphysics (many of the things that she shares in this book), and came back together and shared how our views were shifting. We kept an open mind, even when we felt that our own views were being stretched, once again, by the other. I don't know if I would have found the courage without Marie's ability to trust the loving process of expansion.

It's been more than 15 years since my worldview was totally altered, and as terrifying as it's been, I wouldn't trade it for anything because the fruit of inner transformation is always love. Jesus said that you would know them (his followers) by their fruit. Fruit doesn't lie. It is what it is. And you'll know if the path you're following is a good one for you, depending on whether or not you are growing in love.

There is an abundant harvest of good fruit in our lives. Marie and I are both more open, compassionate, and loving people now and only small traces of fear remain in our lives where fear used to dominate. Our worlds are expansive, and we are more likely to be found reveling in some new discovery about the Universe than staying confined to our beliefs in the way life should be, or heaven forbid, to be found people pleasing. We had to give that up a long time ago, for this wild journey isn't for the tame soul (no soul really is after all!), and the further we go on our adventurous wanderings, the more we see people on the shore waving from a safe distance.

At some point along our journeys, we each decided to live wholeheartedly and to experience the Divine in ways that our minds couldn't previously conceive. Sometimes, that means walking the path for a few solitary miles until another sojourner, one who understands such things, joins you.

I implore you, dear reader, to take heart and to take the journey. Even if no one else can gather the courage to join you, consider Marie a fellow traveler and friend, one who understands and offers this resource, which is an invaluable guide to finding your way to living loved.

~ Julie Calvez Stinson, Intuitive Coach

INTRODUCTION

How this book found me (the author):
Through the decades of my life various friends, coaches, and clients have told me that I had books inside of me, that I was here to communicate and ease the way for others on the journey. I would laugh with skepticism, or sigh in frustration, depending on the day. I couldn't help myself for I knew how challenged I was in the arena of communication, and writing thoughts down was next to impossible for me—until it wasn't.

Growing up, my communication skills were mostly limited to a few key phrases (and swear words when no adults were around.) One day at a family gathering, when we were adults, I asked three of my brothers what I said most often when we were young. In unison they said, "Shut up and who cares!" We had a good laugh, yet it illustrates how deeply stunted I was in my verbal and emotional expression. My childhood challenges, and adult experiences, were the perfect set up to find my authentic self and unique voice. Still, I'd wonder where, when, and if ever, I'd find the courage and skill to speak and write from my soul. The practice of expressing my thoughts clearly came through hundreds of hours with wonderful clients, refining and expanding concepts, with both them and me being transformed in the process.

Years later, in the wee hours of the morning, I recognized that words were flowing and they wanted to be written down. I jumped out of bed to catch the words before they were lost, and five hours later I realized that I had the beginnings of a book – this book. The flow continued day and night for several months, allowing for breaks so regular life could happen. I was amazed that when the time finally came to write, I couldn't help myself! It felt like a sweet gift. The words poured out as and when they would, and I was there to catch them on note paper or napkins, and on the computer. The ideas expressed here came from my soul, and I'll cheerfully lay claim to any errors you find (especially punctuation!). There is always safe room to grow within Love Itself.

May you be blessed in the reading of Living Loved: a path to peace.

A COLORFUL METAPHOR:

Long, long ago and not too far from here, there was a world with four nations. The North Nation was a land of adventure. The people loved to explore and go on quests—anything to experience excitement. The people of the North had eyes that saw everything through the color red. Clouds, sea and people were all various shades of red.

The East Nation was a peaceful people who looked inside to explore and discover new vistas. They were an old and wise people who looked into the deep mysteries of life. They saw everything through the color blue. The rocks, trees, and animals were various shades of blue.

The South Nation people loved to laugh and dance. They delighted in language and created twisting rhymes that tickled the tongue. Golden yellow, blazing with fun, tinged everything they saw. The grass, mountains, and the newborn babies to the eldest poets were tinged with golden yellow.

The West Nation was a serious, hard-working people who valued progress and industry. If they took the time to notice anything besides work, they might have said that everything was brown. All was dreary, to say the least. However, it was their color, and the only one that existed.

When the people of the four nations tried to gather they would soon become confused. Even though they spoke the same language, they couldn't understand one another, for one spoke of red trees, people, and roads, while another declared them to be yellow, and so on. As you may imagine, irritation arose because each was certain there was only one true color, not these variations, and everyone else was wrong. In their attempts to prove themselves right, they became furious and tried to force others to their way of seeing. Cruel wars were the result of this confusion.

A quiet revolution began when the mystical souls of the four nations' people proclaimed they could not only see the other three colors, they could see hundreds more. In large and small ways, they revealed that Love Itself (another name for God) was the key to seeing all the colors. One by one, and soon many more, the people's eyes were opened by love, and their worldviews expanded to see the beauty of a full-color world. The people eventually became more curious and accepting and were united by love. Wars ceased and peace reigned.

This book is about remembering what was forgotten. Living loved is a call for opening to curiosity and expanding our world-views until we are indeed living loved and loving one another in a full-color world.

"Imagine what seven billion humans could accomplish
if we all loved and respected each other. Imagine."
~ A.D. Williams

"You must learn a new way to think
before you can master a new way to be."
~ *Marianne Williamson*

Living Loved means living from a space
of KNOWING you are loved,
experiencing everything through that knowing,
and then taking actions
based only on the wisdom and compassion of that love.
~ Marie Maguire

LIVING LOVED (A POEM)

I envision a world on the path to peace
where we are all safe to explore, to
question and to discover
the spirituality that thrills our soul
each of us knowing that Love Itself
(God) will find us there

I envision Love flowing through
the Muslim, Buddhist, Christian, Hindu, and Jew
walking, dancing, and delighting
in the wonders of each other's journey

I envision a world culture of open peaceful hearts
and joyous colorful laughter
with all of us living loved, and loving one another
arm in arm, on our way home

Beloved, come dance with me as we embrace living loved
~ Marie Maguire

Table of Contents

OPENING

"Believe nothing. Entertain possibilities."
~ Caroline W. Casey

THIS WORLD HAS always seemed a bit unbalanced to me, and even more so of late. You may have noticed that the fear and anger have stepped up a few notches, in the name of patriotism no less. If you've lived through the last twenty to eighty years without feeling bewildered and afraid, then you might already be enlightened. As for the rest of us... well this book is for the rest of us.

I'll not be escalating the insanity by proving how deranged things have gotten; you only need watch the news for five minutes to see it. I will, however, focus this work on guiding you through fear to love and all the way to peace, in your life first and foremost, with the hope that a tipping point will cause that love and peace to spill over into the rest of our world.

Even though there are many controversial topics presented hereafter for your curiosity to entertain, I think we may all agree that we all need love. All of us. Moreover, when we choose to feel loved, we also feel safe and peaceful. They are a package deal. Our need for love is so deeply ingrained that when we don't have it, no matter the reason, we get confused in our mind and body and desperate (violent) in our words and actions. If you trust me through the tough topics, then I'll show you how to live loved and land safely at peace.

We will explore many of the subtle ways we have embraced fear and refused peace, how we have spoken with violence (rude, impatient, and unkind) while also saying we want peace. If you are patient through all of the worldview changing topics, if you are willing to be broadminded, then I will show you how to know you are loved, and how to live and take action from that empowered and peaceful place. A life of peace is possible despite external circumstances! I know it's possible because I live it. If you trust me all the way to the end, then you may live it as well.

What I've seen in my own life is that the violence, and the peace, both begin within me. If I want to have peace, I must become the peace. If I would have kindness and respect, I must become that myself. If I want to live on unmovable, peaceful ground, then I must take back all the power I've given away because of fear, and choose to live from love instead. The love I sought was within me. It is in you as well, I promise.

Please read on as if this book is a love letter from me to you, inviting you to open to new ways of living loved.

"Happiness comes from within.
It is not dependent on external
things or on other people.

You become vulnerable and can be easily hurt when
your feelings of security and happiness depend
on the behavior and actions of other people.
Never give your power to anyone else."
- Brian L. Weiss

WHO NEEDS THIS BOOK?

This book is for people who want to give peace a permanent place in their life. They've experienced plenty of fear and suffering, are tired of it, and long to live in a safe and loving world. It's also for those who know people who have suffered and want to support their loved ones with love and compassion. If you haven't experienced fear, and don't know of anyone who has, you may wish to put this book aside until things change.

If you're still reading, I want you to know this book is an invitation to crack open your worldview, embrace ways to leave fear and suffering behind, guide you on the path to peace, and open you to living loved. You needn't agree with any of the worldview expanding ideas that I present. Being curious about the ideas and exploring, "What if this idea were true?" Actively use your imagination to explore, "How would I think, feel, and be different? How would my inner and outer world change? What new actions would be inspired? What else might be possible?" This active exploration on your part may be enough to shift painful suffering and prepare your heart to live loved.

"The important thing is not to stop questioning.
Curiosity has its own reason for existing."
~ Albert Einstein

"Everything that is new or uncommon
raises a pleasure in the imagination,
because it fills the soul with an agreeable surprise,
gratifies its curiosity,
and gives it an idea
of which it was not before possessed."
~ Joseph Addison

HOW TO USE THIS BOOK

I encourage you to journey through this book in the way that best suits your need, temperament, and interest. Some of you may start at the beginning and read one thought a day, or one every week, digging into your experience of the ideas and allowing them to slowly integrate into who you are becoming. Others may jump around as their intuition dictates, delving into and staying on one idea, allowing it to transform and enlighten their soul. You may even speed right through thinking it not so special, maybe even ridiculous, yet finding that ideas come back months, or years, later when you are ready to go deeper. A number of you may even own the book for years and years before it jumps off the shelf at the right moment. Certainly, your way is the best way for you!

"The most beautiful people we have known
are those who have
known defeat, known suffering,
known struggle, known loss,
and have found their way out of those depths."
~ Elisabeth Kubler-Ross

INVITATION AND WARNINGS

These thoughts are for your heartfelt consideration and meditation. I offer no proof, nor am I seeking argument. Indeed, I acknowledge that I may even sometimes be wrong. I don't care. (You read that right.) On a certain portion of most everyone's journey, we get stuck in certitude. We think (we know!) we have God and life all figured out, and anything outside of that box of certainty becomes scary. We fear that if someone has a belief that is different from ours, one of us must be wrong! This kind of fear produces defensiveness, divisiveness, anger, hatred... This fearfulness doesn't allow for a connection to one another or to Love Itself. I invite you to let go of fear and certitude for a time, and explore, "What else is possible?"

The thoughts presented throughout this book may open your mind and shake up your worldview, thus opening your heart along the way. You'll know you're on a worldview changing topic if it riles you up, scares you, or makes you mad. Slow down and take your time on that topic. Do more research. Meditate. Talk it through with others who are also curious. Thoroughly imagine what your life will be like if you embrace the new worldview idea. I invite you to keep the ideas that open your heart, that inspire the expansion of love and peace in your life, and let the rest flow right on through. As you challenge your most basic beliefs, you grow as a spiritual being and your suffering is diminished. Curiosity is a good resource to take along on this journey.

> "Mans fears are fashioned out of the ways
> in which he perceives the world [his worldview].
> ~ Ernest Becker

The first warning is about the temptation to bypass emotional healing. If you're reading another spiritual book with the understandable desire, and all too human effort, to avoid feeling or healing your wounds – this is not that book. You are a spiritual being having a very human experience, which includes all the wounds, heartaches and stages of growth that must be attended to for this human experience to be fully divine. Abuse recovery, codependency, and individuation, to name a few, must be attended to for wellness to be complete.

We live in a fast-paced, want-it-now, get-it-done kind of world. I hear impatience in clients who want their emotional/spiritual wellness journey to respect their deadlines. I know I was impatient. I'm certain that God laughed good-naturedly when I gave him three months to heal me and get me ready to roll. I really thought I was giving a generous time limit! That deadline passed nearly thirty years ago and I'm still on the journey.

There is no going around. You must go through. The healing, wellness, wholeness journey is progressive and you can, if
you want, be guided by love every step of the way. Wholeness
is achieved more easily when you are living loved, so read on!

**The second warning is against the subtle slide into
spiritual violence**. When working with clients I see the
dawning of a new open-hearted knowing on their faces, which
all too often ricochets off them as their mind speeds toward all
the friends, family and lovers who also need to know this new
thing. Stop, STOP! This ricochet may seem innocent and loving, yet it is first a defense mechanism to prevent change, and
second it is the beginnings of pressing your beliefs, your path,
onto others. You are the one who most needs to know this new
thing, and to live it, until the new knowing has transformed
every area of suffering inspired by not knowing it. When you
are truly living the peace and love brought by the new idea,
then others may notice and ask you about it. Only then is it
wise to share what you've learned. Otherwise their journey is
their business, and your only task is to love them on it.

**The third warning is that you get to decide what
is true for you and only you.** When you learn something
new, here or elsewhere, you may be tempted to make it true for
everyone. This seems related to the second warning, yet there
is a subtle difference. In the warning above the person doesn't
let the new information settle in their bones and become real
to them before they want to spread it around. It ricochet's off
and doesn't become fully embraced before they want to spring

it everyone else. In this warning, the new knowing becomes so bedrock real, a core worldview, that you're tempted to make it true for EVERYONE. "If it's true for me, then it must be true for all people. After all, true is true." Nope. As you read on you'll discover why true isn't true for everyone, and how this worldview causes much of the violence in our world.

THINGS YOU GET TO DECIDE FOR YOURSELF
(AND NOT FOR OTHERS)

- God is personal
- There is no God
- Astrology is real
- Faeries show me the way
- All things work together for my good
- It's time to heal my codependence
- And so on...

For instance, you can decide for yourself that a challenging life situation was good for you because it taught you great things and led to a deeper wisdom. You cannot then turn to your friend in the depths of misery and tell her that her suffering is for the best. She will first want to smack you and then run far away from your inconsiderate words and lack of compassion (aka spiritual violence). She alone can decide the outcome of life's challenges. Let her, in the perfect moment for herself, move to the next level of understanding. You may, however, give a quiet hug and model your own new peace of mind, only lovingly answering questions when asked.

Or, you can decide for yourself that Christianity is the path for you. You cannot then turn to your neighbor who is Muslim (Jewish, Buddhist, etc.) and tell them they are on the wrong path. God meets each one of us right where we are and leads us forward in the way that is best for us.

Instead, be the love you want to see in the world. Jesus is love. Buddha is love. Yogananda is love. Quan Yin is love. Baal Shem Tov is love. God is Love Itself. How about you? And, while you're being love, please mind your own spiritual business and leave everyone else free to mind theirs. Anything less is spiritual violence.

Enough with the warnings; let us move forward to the juicy stuff.

"Authentic spirituality is always about changing you.
It's not about trying to change anyone else."
~ Richard Rohr

"The world is changed by your example,
Not your opinion."
~ Paulo Coelho

"Spiritual bullying is not kind or effective.
You can't traumatize yourself (or
others) into enlightenment."
~ Lissa Rankin

WHO AM I?

I'm an artist, writer, spiritual counselor, and hypnotherapist. I hold two unconventional master's degrees, one of which is in Christian counseling psychology (pastoral). The other is in graphic design, which has nothing to do with anything we will talk about! I also have extensive training in clinical hypnotherapy and neurolinguistic programming (NLP). I'm a human being who once lived deep within fear, and believed that the struggles and heartaches of my life were because of other people and difficult circumstances.

I've also done numerous fear-filled things in my confused attempts to obtain love and safety. Those attempts didn't work. I know they didn't because I tried them several times to be certain. I do like to be certain!

Having survived an extensive spiritual "dark night of the soul," my own worldview was broken open, and I now believe things I would have thought to be absolutely crazy a few years ago. However, the "me" of today is living with more love, peace, and delight than the "me" of years ago. What I believed then was good and just right for the time, yet it wasn't all that was required to heal my body, mind, and soul. Inspired by pain, I opened my heart and mind, discovered new possibilities, expanded my worldview, and found the way out of suffering.

If you need to have a spiritual frame of reference for me, the best labels might be; Christian Mystic, Zen Buddhist, and

Sufi, who also adores Paramahansa Yogananda (read: Christian, Buddhist, Muslim, and Hindu). On my spiritual journey, I've learned to hold a balance in all areas of life, especially between Eastern and Western philosophical and spiritual thought. My passion is to assist others to live, love, and work from a place of emotional and spiritual freedom.

My journey, from closed conservative religion to open spirituality, was arduous and frightening. However, it was also important training, and I learned much about fear, love, and compassion along the way.

I am a sitting mountain,
A laughing stream, a radiant sun,
And the quietness of a comforting moon.
~ Marie Maguire

How Did I Come to Know These Things?

There once was a girl, a sweet enchanted, mystical girl, who was dropped into a sports (football, baseball, basketball, and golf) family with five brothers! She grew up thinking there must have been some mistake with her placement in this family. Maybe the stork got it wrong? Maybe there was a family somewhere that was a better fit for her? Maybe there was a home that would have been quieter, easier, safer, and more respectful of her nature?

This girl's life journey, especially the suffering, inspired her to expand her understanding. She passed the age of fifty before she realized that she'd been dropped into the correct home and that her family had done everything right to help her become who she needed to be today. She realized there were no mistakes, no victims, and no regrets. Upon this realization, she felt only a deep gratitude. Sigh! It was a relief to finally accept and honor all that had come before.

I am that girl, and I have told myself many stories about my experiences along the way. My stories included various forms of abuse, lack of physical safety, disrespect and disregard for my feelings and needs, mentally ill and dangerous people, years spent in conservative religion, divorce, early loss of my parents, "dark night of the soul," raising children, the confusion of abuse recovery, *many* confused attempts to get love, the judgment and rejection of others, and the interesting journey toward spiritual freedom and emotional wellness. I now know that I was born into the right family, with the right personality, and with the right combination of strengths, challenges, and gifts. My upbringing was the perfect set up for me to learn what I needed to know to be the Marie that I am today and to fulfill my mission in this life. Any seeming blunders (lots of confused actions) turned out to be vital steps on my dance to freedom, and I'm grateful for all of my teachers along the way!

Any anecdotes I share in this book are from my own personal stories and experiences. The essence of each story is intact, while details may have been changed to protect others' privacy. I've also learned much from my work of helping people find their own peace of mind, and I write with that understanding, which I trust comes through in what I share. If you want to hear from my clients, please see the testimonials at the end of this book. Also, I share many of my favorite quotes because, as Michel de Montaigne so wisely states, "I quote others only in order (to) better express myself."

You'll find bits of my story sprinkled throughout this book. However, I realize it may not be enough to satisfy anyone's healthy curiosity, so here is a brief memoir to give you a taste of my own messy passage from confusion to love. I hope to share more of my journey should we have the privilege to meet at some future event.

> *"Ring the bells that still can ring*
> *Forget your perfect offering.*
> *There is a crack in everything,*
> *That's how the light gets in."*
> ~ Leonard Cohen

A BRIEF MEMOIR

Imagine growing up without any personal boundaries. No borders, no margins to tell you where you begin and end and no guidelines for how to safely navigate your world. I don't have to imagine it. I lived it for years and years, until I didn't. Without boundaries relationships were messy. I didn't know what was me/not me, good/not good, or safe/not safe. No matter what society teaches, or what churches judge, if an individual has not had the experience of developing healthy boundaries they don't and can't act as if they have them. Once I knew what a boundary was, I vowed to do whatever it took to have healthy boundaries! The thing is, developing boundaries and becoming real is often incredibly messy, and yet the internal and external disarray is worth the ultimate outcome of a healthy life!

There are no villains in the following story, only souls confused about what is right, good and loving.

LITTLE GIRL LOST
My chin rested on my bent knees as I held the wardrobe door closed. I was wedged in the small space, with yarn wrapped around the door-catch as well as my four year old fist. I held the yarn tight because it was keeping the door closed and me safe inside. I barely breathed in the stale cedar-scented air and prayed for help. I wanted to disappear. The only problem was that the predator was already living inside my own head, as well as in my home. Terror gripped my insides. You'd think that I would have been crying right there in the dark, yet I wasn't. I had swallowed most of my emotions long ago and now showed only a false face to the world. My nickname was "Smiley," and I was not at all a happy child.

After I outgrew the tiny wardrobe, I found other spaces to hide that protected my mind when my body was busy elsewhere.

I found a secret trap door in my closet floor that led to an in-between place. This space was cozy, warm, and had lots of cushions. The light was gentle and the silence was delicious. I "ate" to my heart's content and enjoyed all the imaginary meat, potatoes, bread, and bacon I ever wanted. It was a Marie-only space. My secret. My safety.

I also found new homes for me to "live in" where I felt cherished, admired and, more importantly, seen. I lived in the past at the Ponderosa with my wonderful Cartwright family, where I was adored by my brothers and my dad. I lived in the future with my Star Trek family who helped me explore all the mysterious possibilities of who I could become. I wasn't always safe in my imagined adventures, yet I was always heard and respected there.

My very first memory in this life is of my Grandma Chapman's home, a home that was sold when I was a toddler. A party was going on and the home was full of family. The gentle smell of baby powder wafted around me as my diapered bottom bounced down the narrow steep stairs. Again and again, my daring little soul enjoyed this solitary slide down the stairs, starting at the landing and ending at the front coat closet. Eventually becoming bored with that adventure, I made my way all the way up the stairs. At the top, I turned the corner to explore the mystery of this quiet space. All other sounds were muffled except what came through a door down the hall. Like the smell of pollen draws bees to a flower, the laughter drew me on. I swung the door open and to my delight it led to a balcony overlooking the yard full of family. My little hands held the wood slats and my face pressed to the space between to peer below. To my horror the rail began to give way. It stopped with me leaning over the yard miles below. I couldn't move for fear that it would finish falling down and down at any moment. My howl of terror must have caught my dad's ears for he was there in a flash. My relief was momentary however, as he decided to hold me over the balcony, with a catch and release motion, laughing at my renewed terror. All sense of safety exploded in that moment, and all future ideas about love and relationship were twisted upside down. Dad put me down so he and mom could fight about what had just happened. I crawled away to a corner of my Grandma's room, where Grandma later found me silently curled in a fetal position. She sat us down in a rocking chair, held me close, and hummed Brahms's Lullaby. I felt the kindness and comfort being offered, yet it did nothing to fix the twisted and confused worldview that had already formed in me. The daring child was gone; she was replaced by one full of fear.

My Grandma's maiden name was Marie Frances McGuire and she is one of my heroes. My dad, as you may imagine, was not my hero. Fast forward thirty years, and one of my brothers called asking me what he could do differently so his own daughter wouldn't hate him "like you hated dad." I calmly answered his question, put down the phone, and repeated, "I hated my dad? I hated my dad..." over and over with a swelling surge until the long held dam burst. The rage came first as I found the flaming river that had burned through the underground chasm of my life. Next, the ice shield over my numb emotions thawed and I cried a bucket of tears.

Admitting that I hated my dad and shedding long pent up tears was a key turning point in my life; however, I had a long, long way to go. Abuse recovery, in my thirties, was a powerful experience that transformed many aspects of my inner world. What I needed next was to form healthy boundaries. Unfortunately, they don't magically appear. I developed them over the next several years by discovering all the ways to not do relationships—all kinds of relationships. This process was painful for me, my children and for many others.

LOST GIRL FOUND

The early morning sleepy calm exploded with sound. Boom, boom, crash! The pounding on the door reverberated throughout that old house. Someone was screaming and kicking at the front door. A heartbroken woman was after her wayward husband, the one in my bed who had told me his marriage was over. Apparently not. My poor sweet daughter, home from college, came out of her room wide-eyed with terror. I felt horrified and ashamed for I knew that, once again, I had been gullible and believed another lie. Even so, my heart was already entangled and it took a while to unravel the messy knot.

Sometime later I met a single man (an improvement) who was gallantly struggling with a life-threatening illness. He began paying attention to me and showing up at unlikely places.

My heart would flutter and dream. Maybe we could be together for the short time he had left. Even a good-hearted romance, however brief, was better and healthier than anything else I had experienced. We dated delightfully for a short time until the truth came out that....wait for it....he wasn't really ill. He'd made the whole thing up for attention. The charade was a desperate action inspired by an emotional disorder. There goes my healthier romance. That's it. I quit!

I felt dizzy from the merry-go-round of emotions and broken hearts. Three divorces, two additional marriage proposals in relationships later gone awry, and numerous other attempts to connect. I'd twisted myself every which way so I could finally feel safe and worthy of love. Instead I felt like trash and wondered where I was going wrong. Would I ever have clear vision or healthy instincts?! I felt like a worthless God-damn-fucking-moron with shit for brains! (My apologies to those offended by swear words. That's how I used to talk to myself before I learned how to live loved.)

In the midst of my boundary development phase I met a woman who would develop into a deep soul friend. I remember the look in her eyes early in the relationship, her head tilted up and away from me as if she didn't know what to make of this writhing, miserable, and cursing creature. I could see her perplexity and yet she didn't run away. She told me later that she was intrigued: "Here was a woman who obviously loved God, and yet felt safe enough within that love to be authentically messy." Really, really messy! Julie (whom you've met in the forward to this book) didn't turn away from our friendship because, as she stated, I had the very thing she longed for: authenticity. We became friends over twenty years ago. In that time I have modeled courage and she has shown light on my way. Side by side we became and are becoming what we never could have accomplished alone. I thank God every day that we found one another along the way.

To me it isn't amazing that I've lived such a messy, confused journey. My childhood experiences and decisions were the perfect set up for a messy adult life. What does amaze me is that there were so many vibrant parts of me that were healthy and sane. I've healed the wounded parts, cleared up the confusions and, with the help of many loving friends, have labored to build an authentic life based in Love Itself.

"Reject the brutal, reject the beauty."
~ Glennon Doyle Melton

*"My story isn't sweet and harmonious,
like invented stories.
It tastes of folly and bewilderment, madness and dream,
like the life of all people who no longer want
to lie to themselves."*
~ Hermann Hesse

*"Once you are real you can't become
unreal again. It lasts for always."*
~ Margery Williams

EXPANDING YOUR WORLDVIEW

"People don't change," is a commonly held maxim.
I'd like to offer a different view: People don't change
UNLESS they heal the root confusion
that caused the unhealthy behavior.
Once the confusion is cured,
wonderful things are possible!

THOUGHTS ON YOUR WORLDVIEW

Since opening and expanding your worldview is the first step on the path to peace, it might be helpful to know what a worldview is and how it's developed. A worldview is your personalized container for what things mean, how things work, who you are, whether the world is a safe place, and how to get your needs met. It comprises and defines your own particular reality and helps you make sense of your surroundings. Your personal worldview began developing in the womb and was created by your decisions about who you are and how the world works, cultural and religious training, temperament type, brain dominance, education, and a multitude of experiences. **Your worldview influences how you interpret and react to**

everything around you. Imagine it as the personalized filtered lens through which you see and experience everything. In this book, we'll explore how your worldview can cause your fear and suffering and how to change it, so that you may fully embrace living loved.

Your worldview is essentially invisible and stays invisible, until the pain it causes gets your attention and inspires you to seek a remedy. There are several worldview ideas that may cause you to be fearful and suffer. Some of those ideas include:

- Life should be easy and smooth. (Where's my white picket fence?!)
- The world isn't a safe place, so I must grab up safety wherever I can find it.
- It isn't acceptable to be an introvert (gay, short, bald, a different race, etc.)
- I'm not enough. I'm unlovable.
- I need more money to feel safe.
- I'm too loud (quiet, strong, gentle, sensitive, etc.)
- I only get to live once, so I fear and hide from death.
- To make it in this world I must stifle my soul and be socially acceptable.
- God is demanding and harsh (or there is no God).
- I'm on my own and need power to survive (or belong).

It takes only a little imagination to follow these thoughts down to the suffering they cause. Let's choose one and briefly see where it takes us: **Life should be easy and smooth**. As with all worldviews, you would find this idea by the shadow it casts over your life. You might be depressed by the "never ending challenges," or be asking, "Why does "it" (job, relationship, etc) hurt so much?" You may even find yourself attempting to drown this belief in an addiction, or threatening to give up altogether. The way to turn "easy and smooth" around is to find a worldview that is more truthful and life affirming for you, such as: Life is an adventure to be lived and enjoyed. Or, Life is an opportunity to try different ways of living. Or, I've lived before and will live again and it's all for fun and for learning. When you allow one, or all, of these new worldviews to sink down into your bones you begin seeing and interpreting experiences through a brighter more positive lens.

The good news is that you're not stuck with your worldviews; they can expand, shift, and change altogether, as you explore new ideas, and be open to what else is possible? The possibilities are endless for finding a more enjoyable worldview that changes how you view and interpret the adventures coming your way. All through this book, you will discover ways to expand, yet, before we dive in, let's first find out how you keep your worldview small and closed.

WAYS TO EVADE WORLDVIEW EXPANSION:

- You avoid reading, or only read books from one narrow genre.
- You don't travel or watch TV shows about travel.

- You reject friendship with people of other beliefs and cultures.
- You keep your habits of living very small by never trying anything new.
- You don't explore other spiritual or religious traditions.
- You argue every difference of opinion (worldview).
- You make fun of or judge anyone who is different from you.
- You believe every thought that goes through your mind.
- You avoid discomfort and make all decisions from fear.
- You shun those who seem to bring discomfort to your life (those who don't agree with you).
- You choose to live with a closed and angry heart.

Now, if you weren't open to expanding your worldview, I'm fairly confident you wouldn't still be reading this book. I sincerely admire your courage for reading and exploring the idea of expanding your worldview.

The important thing to note is that **every single time you suffer your suffering is contained within and defined by one of the beliefs within your worldview**. Not just sometimes, always; no matter how you may try to blame someone else! The good news about your suffering being contained within your worldview is that you have complete control over your worldview contents.

For suffering to cease, your worldview must expand or change altogether.

I ENCOURAGE YOU TO:

- Notice when and where there is suffering in your life, (fear, anger, resentment, verbal or emotional violence, impatience, unkindness, etc.)
- Discover your limiting beliefs (worldviews).
- State your willingness for it/them to be transformed.
- Ask for and expect spiritual guidance (angel, soul friend, coach).
- Enlarge your heart and mind by exploring other possibilities.
- Choose a new, joyous, and loving worldview,
- Declare it to be true for you.
- Meditate on the new worldview day and night.
- And begin living (speaking and acting) as if you believe it – until you do!

No ethical spiritual guide is going to tell you this process is fast or easy. Nonetheless, it is worth it! Releasing what no longer serves you, and embracing what opens your understanding, are what healing and wellness are all about.

Releasing painful worldviews is an essential step to opening your heart and mind to living loved. Embrace new worldviews, actively participate in creating a happier life, and if you're persistent, you'll even discover the joy of living loved.

Please note: At the end of most sections I'll be pointing out possible old worldviews that cause suffering and suggesting new worldviews that lead to feeling loved. I invite you to expand on these ideas using your own personal worldviews that need to change and adding new ones that make you feel safe and loved. Make your additions as positive, loving and empowering as you wish!

Most people do not see their beliefs [worldview].
Instead, their beliefs tell them what they see.
This is the simple difference between
clarity and confusion.
~ Matt Kahn

"Your pain is the breaking of the shell
that encloses your understanding."
~ Kahlil Gibran

Fear of Expansion

Our worldviews were decided and designed by us (most are developed before the age of seven), so they fit quite comfortably, right up until they don't. Those who share our similar worldviews are comfortable as well, and may not want anyone changing or rearranging the shared zone. Some of our friends and family could even use scare tactics to keep us within this shared worldview. There might be fear, anger, hurt, threat of hellfire, and maybe eventually shunning in an attempt to keep you contained, for awhile.

And yet, growth, once inspired, will not be ignored. Sometimes, there's an internal pressure, a curiosity, an insatiable desire to know more. There's skepticism about rules and limitations, severe suffering, or even a longing for more love and peace. Whatever the reason, there comes a moment when it is more painful to stay where you are than to open and explore. Keep moving forward and trust love to lead you safely through.

I can't and don't guarantee that expanding your worldview won't contribute to the loss of jobs, family members, or lifelong friends. It sometimes happens, and you're the one who has to decide when you're ready, willing, and able to grow, and what price you're willing to pay.

"And the day came
when the risk to remain tight in a bud
was more painful
than the risk it took to blossom."
~ Anais Nin

The lobster has much to teach us about how to expand. When it grows and its hard shell becomes too tight and uncomfortable, it finds a safe place to shed the old and grow the new. One of the key features of living as if you are loved is trusting that you will be guided, and held safely, while you shed the old and grow the new. You may wander for awhile, yet you will never be lost.

WHAT IF …

- Curiosity is honored in the spiritual realms?
- Love Itself allows you the freedom to explore, and find your own way, in your own time?

- Your uniqueness is so cherished that you're invited to dance through life in the way that makes sense to you?
- Following a particular spiritual or religious brand (the only right way to God) doesn't matter because God will travel any path to find you?

I'm inviting each of you to be curious and ask, "What will life be like when I open my heart to new ideas?" Allow yourself to feel and experience your way through each of these presented ideas, and discover what new peace, hope, and love might be awaiting you. Allow love to be the touchstone for your life's decisions, and know that when you follow love, it will always lead you safely to your own heart and home to Love Itself.

"We can easily forgive a child who is afraid of the dark:
the real tragedy of life is when men
are afraid of the light."
~ Plato

"Every time you tear a leaf off a calendar,
you present a new place for new ideas and progress."
~ Charles Kettering

ALL IS LOVE OR FEAR
It seems a bit simplistic to say that everything we think and every action we take can be boiled down to its most basic motivation. Nevertheless, I've found it to be true. The motivation

may be summed up as either fear or love. I don't expect you to believe this idea because I said it. I invite you to check it out for yourself. The next time, and every time, you think, feel, or decide something, ask yourself whether it is based on love or fear. If you can't find the words "fear" or "love" in your answer, ask if this thought, feeling, or decision, makes your life feel bigger, brighter, and more energized, or if it makes your life feel smaller, darker and less energetic? *Love is expansive. Fear is limiting.*

When you are faced with a thought, feeling, or decision, you have the option of approaching the thought, etc., from a place of love or fear.

Fear says no, never, that's too hard, I won't be loved, it's not fair, my friends will reject me, or bad things will happen. Sometimes fear can push you forward into actions that are founded in "should," "could," or "ought to," and bids for approval. Fear shows up in a smaller life, an unwillingness to try again, or it even disguises itself as wisdom with its cautionary tales of woe or rational reasons to avoid what love tells us to do. You may even think that fear-based actions will protect you. Yet, with fear-based actions, the heart and body shrivel as the years go by and you may become lonely, depressed, and physically ill.

Love says yes, and yes again. I will love. I will remain open to hope. No matter what happens I will trust in love. At times, love inspires us forward into bold actions founded in faith, inspiration, and even blind obedience to Love Itself. Love knows that it is always safe, so it can move into a bigger life and be willing to try again and again. It has a quiet wisdom that is open and kind. It doesn't need to defend, explain itself, or judge others. Love-based actions never harm another, though they may require bravery and trust. When love says no, it is with a quiet confidence that another, better door will open at the right time. Love leads us to oneness, wellness, and peace.

Old worldview

- I'm not safe. The world isn't a safe place.
- Fear is just trying to keep me safe.
- I should listen to and act on fear-based thinking.

New worldview

- I am safe within Love Itself.
- Love leads me forward with wisdom.
- I listen only to the wisdom of love.
- I take only empowered action.
- Love does no harm to myself or others.

"It seems... there are only two choices... Fear - Or - Love.
Except when we choose fear it's more like a 'do-over'.
The universe just repeats the pattern as many
times as we need until love is chosen.
That means there is truly just one choice...LOVE."
~ Rikka Zimmerman

Different Kinds of Fear
The word fear is used in many ways, so let's explore a few different kinds of fear and learn what to do with each one.

There is a spark of fear that ignites when your wild instinctive nature says that danger is near. This kind of fear calls for immediate action, with the intent of saving your life. Pay attention to this kind of fear, and take action! However, if you have injured instincts, the call-for-action process may be a bit haywire. You may need assistance to heal your instinctive nature. I know from personal experience that it's a journey well worth taking.

EVIDENCE OF INJURED INSTINCTS:

- Staying too long when a job or relationship is injuring you.
- Allowing others to treat you with disrespect.
- Living a life path assigned to you rather than choosing one for yourself.
- Filling up with food/drugs/sex when what you need is self-love and self-respect.
- Taking responsibility for others' feelings or actions.
- Not recognizing and firmly handling internal and external predators.
- Not letting "No" (yours or others) be a complete sentence.
- Analyzing and talking yourself out of your deep inner wisdom.

HEALING TIPS:

- Embrace authenticity: Take all the time you need to get to know who *you* are by journaling favorites: smells, tastes, sounds, sights, etc. Discover your temperament type; explore your astrology birth chart and numerology profile to round out your knowledge. List what thrills your soul and go do more of it. If you don't know what thrills you then go on a series of expeditions to find out! Celebrate and honor what you find.
- Explore and embrace many of the worldview expanding ideas presented in this book.
- Get the help of a coach or counselor for setting new boundaries.
- Read *The Gift of Fear* by Gavin DeBecker to regain trust in your intuitive knowing.
- Read *Women Who Run with the Wolves* by Clarissa Pinkola Estés to learn about healing your wise instinctive self.
- More and more often, take action when your inner voice tells you what is best.

Then there's a type of fear (worry/anxiety) that tells you that you're not enough. This fear seems to be a generalized project that many people are working on at this time. It's a spotlight shining on a worldview inside of you that needs to be healed. Follow that fear to heal it so you may move forward with grace.

Marianne Williamson says that "our deepest fear is not that we are inadequate. Our deepest fear is that we are powerful beyond measure." Again, this kind of fear calls for inner work to remove all obstacles to living in the full light of love. You'll know this one is healed when you move forward with joyous confidence.

Finally, the kind of fear that I'll be mentioning throughout this book is fear that calls for limitation, the closing of heart and mind, the refusal to wonder or be curious. It wants to be safe and right so badly that it grabs onto one option and shouts, "NO!" to all the other wonders and available resources. It's accurate to say that this type of fear creates a worldview that inspires and contains all of your suffering, and therefore, it needs to be gently opened and cleared out so that Love Itself may flood in and fill you with peace. Again, this healing path is worthy of pursuit.

What kinds of fear are active in your life and what will you do now? Keep asking yourself, what else is possible?

Old worldview

- I won't be safe if I don't listen to all my feelings of fear.
- All fear is wise and I need to follow its advice.

New worldview

- Paying attention to intuitive/instinctive (true) fear may save my life.
- All other fears show me what needs to be healed.

- I only follow fear (worry/anxiety) when I intend to heal my heart, mind and soul.
- Love will lead me safely through every challenge.

"1. When you feel fear, listen.
2. When you don't feel fear, don't manufacture it.
3. If you find yourself creating worry,
explore and discover why."
~ Gavin DeBecker

The only time we must follow the other kinds of fear
is to discover what part of us needs love and healing.
~ Marie Maguire

"Just as love brings profound healing
to our relationships,
Understanding brings a lessening of fear.
As we let go of fears, the obstacles to love disappear,
and love flows freely within, and
between, and among us."
~ Dr. Brian Weiss

WHAT IS LUCID LIVING?

Maybe you have experienced, or heard about, lucid dreaming. With lucid dreaming, one wakes up lightly enough within a dream to know that you are still dreaming. You may even choose to consciously play with, explore, and influence how the dream turns out.

Lucid living is when you wake up enough within your life to realize that this life as (your name here) is another kind of dream. You have dreamed before and will dream again. It's realizing that the form you present (gender, race, personality, etc.) in this particular dream is temporary and has a purpose. When you are lucid within this life, you discover that you are here for fun and learning and you decide to relax and enjoy yourself along the way. You know at a deep level that all is well no matter what happens along the way in this dream time.

WHEN YOU PRACTICE LUCID LIVING:

- You wake up within this life and cease blaming anyone for how they've treated you, for what was said, or for how things are progressing.
- You stop being in a hurry or being afraid of what will happen next.
- You may even realize that everyone within this life as (fill in your name) is part of you and has a good message for you if you are willing to listen.
- You acknowledge that you chose the lessons you wanted to learn in this lifetime and that everyone you meet is here to help you grow and learn those lessons for your own spiritual growth.
- You realize that you will dream again and again, with a new form, new gender, and new challenges, and it's all for fun and for learning.

When you wake up within this dream that you call life, you will declare it to be perfect! When you experience emotional suffering it's because you have gone back to sleep, and you are buying into something that is fear-based and untrue. May you choose, at the right moment for you, to wake up and stay awake!

Old worldview

- The world I see is the only reality.
- I am an unlucky victim of circumstances.
- Others are to blame for my suffering.

New worldview

- There is much more going on than I currently see.
- I am curious about how I have created my world.
- I wake up more and more in this life as (insert name).
- What if I chose this particular life and challenge?

DIFFERENCE BETWEEN FACT AND STORY

In my conversations with clients and friends, I notice confusion about what is fact and what is story. I invite you to open to the possibility of a vast difference between the two that, when embraced, will transform your life. It did mine. Embracing this difference is one key to the end of mental, physical, and emotional suffering so that you may easily move down the path toward peace.

A fact is basic, unadorned, indisputable information.

SOME EXAMPLES OF FACTS ARE:

1. Man sitting in chair
2. Woman is let go from a job
3. Child dies in accident
4. Marriage dissolves in divorce

A story is *anything* that is added to the fact, such as descriptions, judgments, projections, or conclusions. A story is always disputable because it's based on each individual's internal state of being.

SOME EXAMPLES OF STORY ADDED TO THE FACTS AS STATED ABOVE ARE:

1. The man in the chair is a lazy, good-for-nothing liar.
2. I can't stand it. It isn't fair losing this job! This job loss is the worst thing that could've happened at this time.
3. The child's death was a terrible tragedy. He should've lived many more years.
4. The divorce was all her fault. If she had been more _____ they would still be married.

The stories you add to the facts give clear evidence of your own fear-based beliefs and the content of your worldview. **Your stories are about you, and only you, even if you use**

someone else's name as the lead character. Like a magnifying glass your stories amplify and reveal the parts of yourself that need healing. Questioning those stories, using some form of inquiry, is the surest way out of suffering.

To put it mildly, I resisted inquiry. I didn't want to question my stories. I wanted to keep them! They were the way I made sense of the world. Finally, after intense suffering, I'd had enough. I found the courage to question the stories I was adding to the facts. And, until I gained enough ground to do it on my own, I did it with the help of a practitioner. In the process, I discovered that it was me, and only me, causing my suffering. The pain was merely the trigger that revealed the suffering contained within my worldview.

I truly find inquiry to be the surest, fastest, and cleanest way out of suffering. I share more on this topic in another section of this book.

Old worldview

- All my stories are true.
- How I interpret the world is the only truth.
- It is right to believe everything I think.
- It makes me angry and scared to think my stories aren't true.
- Stories presented by the news media are always true.

New worldview

- I don't know anything for sure.
- There are many ways to interpret circumstances.

- My stories are all about what's going on inside of me.
- My stories reveal parts of me that need to heal.
- When I'm seeing clearly then empowered action is easy.
- The news media presents stories to influence my worldview.

"Spiritual maturity is when you spare
yourself hours of suffering
by not taking anything personally."
~ Julie Calvez Stinson

"When I have a thought about you,
that is something I've created.
I've turned you into an idea. In a certain sense,
if I have an idea about you that I
believe, I've degraded you.
I've made you into something very small. . . .
this is what we do to each other."
~ Adyashanti

DIFFERENCE BETWEEN PAIN AND SUFFERING

Pain happens to all of us: birth, death, injuries, accidents, crime, loss, and grief. Pain may also be about growing and expanding in your life. Pain comes to release you of all that's not alive or no longer serves your best interest.

The funny thing about pain is that when you resist, it gets worse. When you relax and breathe into the pain, everything gets easier and there is less pain. Pain is a part of life while in the body and may even be an indication of exciting growth!

Suffering is an option. And it's an option you can learn to live without. Suffering is that internal misery, agony, or torment you feel inside. It is the direct result of believing the fearful stories you create (adding to the facts) and repeat in your mind. The core of these stories is inspired entirely by your worldview content. Changing your worldview stories is the only permanent way to end your suffering.

My friends, it is possible to have pain and not suffer. Keep reading to discover how this misery-free life is achievable.

HERE ARE SOME COMMON STORIES THAT CAUSE SUFFERING:

- Things should be different.
- I need things to be different for me to be happy.
- She should love me.
- I need my family to understand me.
- I need you to be nice to me.
- Life isn't fair.
- He was so rude to me.
- Good people don't have this much trouble.
- My childhood should have been different.

HERE ARE SOME OF MY EXAMPLES GENERALIZED:

1. You break your fingers in an accident (pain). You tell yourself that this accident is unfair and inconvenient, and ask how a loving God could allow this agony to happen (suffering). It's someone else's fault (blame and suffering). Or, you could be with what is (broken fingers) without adding any meaning or story to the event. Ow!

2. Your car stops dead at the side of the road. Now, here is an opportunity for a lot of the suffering contained in your worldview to show itself. Certainly, you could let yourself be curious about what is contained in those internal suffering stories in order for them to come out and be healed. Or, you could take a deep breath, accept what is as if it came from Love Itself (trust), and call for assistance.

3. Your mom died when you were 30 years old (pain). Story: She died too young and you're too young to be without a mom (suffering). Or, keep breathing, feel the pain, and let it stay as long as needed. Let grief take its natural course, however long that is for you, without adding unnecessary suffering.

4. You're in a time of transition and it feels scary and confusing. Nothing much seems to be happening, yet there is a feeling of pain inside. You have a choice in what to think about. Suffering thoughts: "I should be different. I must have done something wrong to deserve this fearful change. God is punishing me for past wrongs". Or you could trust that Love Itself is leading you where you need to go. The pain wants to help you release all that

no longer serves you. This transition can be a time of excitement and celebration rather than fear. Living loved is always your choice.

These are only a few examples of the things you can say to yourself to cause tremendous suffering. The wonderful news is that suffering truly is an option. This book is full of tools to bring about the end of your suffering so that you may find the path to peace.

When we believe what we think,
when we take our thinking to be reality, we will suffer.
~ Adyashanti

INQUIRY

One of the great mysteries of life is the question of why human beings resist that which will only make their life better. I have been a "resistant ass" (so named by a truly loving friend), especially when it came to embracing a tool that was key to ending my suffering. Silly me! And, thank God for another kind, and very patient, friend who, again and again, shared her experiences with, and excitement about, inquiry. With her love she finally breached the wall of my resistance.

A great question that I often hear, usually accompanied by a miserable tone, is "why do we have to experience so much pain in this life?" **Resistant ass, meet Mr. Pain = openness for movement and growth.** At least, that is the way that equation has worked for me and every other human being I've worked with. Maybe you will be different!

Inquiry is the ongoing investigation into the trueness of the thoughts that cause you to suffer. It's an opportunity to be completely free of suffering at the hand of your own thoughts. Author Byron Katie presents inquiry, in its most accessible form, as a series of simple straight forward questions. Therefore, when you discover you're enduring any level of suffering, turn to "The Work" questions or seek out a practitioner who may assist you through this powerful process of self-review.

With the help of a facilitator of "The Work," I learned to use the questions to transform my life. They are now a great resource no matter what story comes my way.

Let go of resistance, just like me, and dive into inquiry. The information presented in any of the books by Byron Katie can, if you let it, lead you out of suffering. There are great videos on YouTube and wonderful inquiry worksheets available on Katie's website: www.thework.com.

Old worldview

- All my thoughts are true.
- My harsh and angry thoughts keep me safe.

New worldview

- Most of my thoughts are untrue.
- My thoughts are influenced by my confused worldviews.
- When I question my thoughts they cease to control my life.
- It is possible to stop suffering by questioning my thoughts.
- When I cease believing all my thoughts, my mind gets quiet and peaceful.
- My relationships thrive when I question my thoughts.

"Leave your front door open and your back door open.
Allow your thoughts to come and go.
Just don't serve them tea."
~ Shunryu Suzuki

IS THERE A HELL?

The idea of hell is one of the many controversial topics in this book. I invite you to release, for the moment, everything you believe or think you know about this subject and explore, "What else is possible?" What would your life be like if you entertained the possibility that hell (and heaven, of course) is ever present and experienced in this moment? What if you are creating and living in hell when you suffer, take fear-based actions, or are hurt by the stories in your head? Embrace for this moment, the idea that you are already living in hell when you react to your suffering-filled thoughts as if they are the truth. What if hell is living in fear and believing your thoughts of dread, loss, and separation?

Now, what if you are already living in heaven when you know that, whatever happens, you are held safely in love. You have a higher awareness and understanding of events when you realize that everything that comes your way is for your best and comes through the filter of Love Itself. You know that separation is an illusion and that you are one with all that is. Heaven is Love Itself fully expressed. When Love is chosen, it works its way backward into all the shadowy corners of your life, transforming things for your highest good and causing all things to shine with the light of love.

Within these ideas, hell and heaven are a moment by moment choice. No one sends you there, except you.

Old worldview

- There is a hell where I can be sent.
- Hell is for people who do bad things.
- If God is just, all my enemies will go to hell.

New worldview

- Heaven? Hell? Who knows for sure? No amount of debate will prove anything.
- I daily choose to live in heaven or hell based on my own thoughts and actions.
- Heaven and hell are a moment by moment choice.

- I can leave the hell of suffering anytime I choose.
- I am loved, I am safe, and I know it!
- During and after this life I'll be embraced by Love Itself.

"What a man has made himself he will be;
his state is the result of his past life,
and his heaven or hell is in himself."
~ Catherine Crowe

EMBRACE THE POWER OF AND

I invite you to become ever more conscious of the power of your words. As Albus Dumbledore says, "Words, in my not-so-humble opinion, are our most inexhaustible source of magic." When used unwisely they are also the cause of much suffering to ourselves and to those we love. Take the word "but" for instance:

I love you, <u>but</u> I want to explore new ways to relate to each other.
I love you, <u>and</u> I want to explore new ways to relate to each other.

<u>But</u> is a word that implies an exception. Whatever words you put in front of the word "but" get canceled out completely!

- You're a great friend, but…
- I admire the work you do, but…
- You do a lot around here, but…
- I want to make love, but…

The "but" sentence at the beginning of this section sounds like an ending. The "and" sentence sounds like a fun new beginning. What if we always used the word "and" instead? What will your world be like when you add the word "and" into your thinking and communications? I invite you to be conscious this week, notice all the "buts" being used, and play around with including "and" in your conversations. I wonder how much fun you will have and what new adventures you will create in this life!

Old worldview

• My choice of words doesn't matter.

New worldview

• I have the power to create and destroy based on the words I choose.

EITHER/OR BECOMES AND

An either/or dualistic society has existed for a long, long time, at least since the ancient Greeks. It has deeply influenced us to the core of our worldviews. The challenge of either/or thinking is that it causes separation, even shunning. It separates you from others, from love, from God, and too often from your own inner self. How does it do that? In the extremes of either/or thinking, you place people, jobs, God, or yourself in categories of either all good or all bad. Either you're loveable or you're not loveable.

Either people are reliable or they're not reliable. Either this decision is right or this decision is wrong. People lie or they don't lie. Women are good, men are bad. These extremes cause you to live in an all-or-nothing world that is stressful, fear-based, and unsupportive of physical, emotional, and spiritual health.

Instead of the black and white world of either/or, what if you lived in the full-color world of "and"? "And" embraces both options and includes so much more! You have good traits, and you have traits that call for growth. Everyone falls and rises. You have moments when you are reliable, and you have other moments when you're not reliable. Each and every one of us withholds the truth at some point in our lives. "And" helps you find (and hopefully embrace) your own frailty and foibles so that you may accept and forgive others who are just as delightfully human as you.

Old worldview

- This is an all or nothing world.
- People are either good or bad.
- Black-and-white thinking keeps me safe.

New worldview

- I live in a full-color world.
- I live with an open heart and mind.
- Everyone fails, including me.
- I am so much more than the mistakes I've made.
- I need love and compassion and so does everyone else.

"Thinking is difficult. That's why most people judge."
~ Carl Jung

*"Everybody believes they are the good
guy. The best way to disarm
your enemies is to really listen to them"*
~ Amaryllis Fox

*"Love sometimes wants to do us a great favor:
hold us upside down and shake all the nonsense out."*
~ Hafiz

WHAT ELSE IS POSSIBLE?

I imagine that most of us human beings have experienced the frustrations of swirling thoughts. I know I have; how about you? As the mind circles around a thought, a virtual whirlwind of dualistic thinking is created in the brain and limits your ability to see other possibilities. Either this or that seems the only choice, and often, neither is acceptable. Both options may cause you to suffer. What a miserable dilemma! Fortunately, there is a question that stops the whirlwind, changes your internal state, and opens you up to other ideas. The question is, "What else is possible?" Below are some examples of how to use the "what else is possible" question.

Example: You need your car keys and you've looked everywhere. **Either** they are lost **or** you're an idiot. You could dissolve into calling yourself names or you can breathe and ask, "What else is possible?" Then go do something distracting and let the inspired answer come to you as to the placement of your keys. The answer invariably does come to you.

Example: You and your spouse are opposite in many ways. **Either** you divorce **or** you're miserable. "What else is possible?" What other ways could you create a relationship that honors you both? What needs might you meet for yourself rather than heaping demands on the other?

Example: Your friend says something that hurts your feelings. **Either** they are a narcissist **or** they are intentionally mean. "What else is possible?" Do your own inner healing work. Question your thoughts and give yourself what you need. Then, without blaming or name calling, have a nonviolent conversation about the event. Who knows, your friendship may even grow from this developmental experience.

Example: Your parents (siblings, friends) are different from you and don't understand your needs. **Either** they are self-centered **or** they don't love you. "What else is possible?" They could have completely different temperament types than yours, different love languages, different social needs, different emotional intelligence strengths, etc. There are too many possibilities to name. You are the one who needs to understand you and then learn to ask for what you need.

HERE'S WHAT YOU CAN DO:

1. STOP when you notice the swirling either/or thinking.
2. Breathe and drop your shoulders.
3. Ask, "What *else* is possible?" Maybe even ask this question with laughter and curiosity in your voice.
4. Go do something distracting and trust the answer(s) will come.
5. Explore the other possibilities presented.
6. Take action only from a place of love.

If you find yourself asking, "What else is possible?" quite often then you are right on target.

> *"The words you speak become the house you live in."*
> ~ Hafiz

ANNOUNCING THE END

I don't know about you, but I can take myself and my foibles pretty seriously. One slip up and it feels like a catastrophe. Then, thoughts about the slip-up spiral into a disaster of immense proportions. How does one stop this process of suffering? Put up a billboard!

This billboard is imaginary, huge, and high in the sky and full of neon lights. The billboard content changes with every new slip up.

The world is ending because
I forgot to call my friend!

The world is ending because
the neighbor is upset with me!

The world is ending because
I told my child there is no Santa Claus!

The world is ending because
we decided to divorce!

The purpose of this billboard is to take your fearful thoughts to the extreme, crack you up, and help you see the short-term impact of your action or inaction. After the billboard has done its job you may put it away until the next announcement of world-ending activity. I invite you to tell your friends about the billboard, so they can remind you to put things up there and laugh with you to freedom.

> *"Cousin Jimmy says that a man in Priest Pond says
> the end of the world is coming soon.
> I hope it won't come till I've seen everything in it."*
> ~ L.M. Montgomery

FACING THE WORST:
Sometimes, after you've put the billboard away your thoughts may still trouble you with fear. Maybe it's a possible outcome that is scaring you. Another tool for being free is taking the fear out into the open and asking, "What is the worst that could happen?"

Explore your worst fears and give several possibilities until you arrive at the thought that bothers you the most. As you look at this most feared option, ask yourself, "Would I survive?" Then come up with a practical plan for survival. You may find the fear diminishes to nearly zero. If the feared option is physical death, I invite you to read *The Afterlife of Billy Fingers* by Annie Kagan.

> *"Be at rest once more, O my soul, for*
> *the Lord has been good to you.*
> *(You have) delivered my soul from*
> *death, my eyes from tears,*
> *my feet from stumbling, that I may walk before the Lord*
> *in the land of the living."*
> ~ King David, Psalm 116, NIV

GOD IN OUR OWN IMAGE

The topic of God is cause for much violence and suffering – for the world and for us as individuals. We embrace the mainstream belief of our culture and defend it with violent words and actions, or we may go to the opposite extreme rejecting the idea of God altogether, and blaming belief in Him for the violence, and think following any belief system is ignorant. Wow, lots of room for suffering and living in fear. What if it's all about you?

If you find an aspect of God (or religion) that you don't like, it would benefit you to heal that aspect in yourself. After that inner healing, lo and behold, God is free of it as well.

- God is male and I don't trust men
- God is unreliable and vindictive
- God is never around when I need him/her
- Look at the what the church has/hasn't done
- Believers are selfish and judgmental

> *"Our idea about God*
> *tells us more about ourselves than about Him."*
> ~ Thomas Merton

Example: For years when I would pray, it was common for me to beg God to not "drop me." In my time of abuse recovery, the aforementioned memory came forward of the moment when my dad held me over that balcony, pretending he was going to drop me, laughing at my terror. After healing this pivotal soul wound, I realized that it wasn't God who was threatening to drop me. It wasn't him laughing at my fear. I was immediately free of that prayer and the accompanying fear. God became much more reliable and safe.

Example: Somewhere in my old worldview I believed that God was only tolerating me and that He had a biting sense of humor. This fear-based idea was cleared up as I continued my healing journey and discovered that this view was created by my experience of my dad and other people in my life. God, Love Itself, is kind, gentle and respectful of me and my needs.

Example: Every church I've ever attended was full of human beings with all the frailties and faults that go along with being human. I was one of them. These institutions and human souls presented me with countless opportunities to grow, find my voice, and work through my own bad attitudes. And I presented the same opportunity to them. Being a follower of any religious system does not stop a person from being human. Love Itself invites each of us to keep growing together and as individuals.

Example: I'm sure I'm not alone in this next one. I believed that God had a rather low opinion of women. What I grew up hearing was that women are stupid, women are bad drivers, women are worthless, and so on. Most of this was spoken under the guise of humor, of course. When I learned that God is the balance of all things, including feminine and masculine traits, I couldn't imagine that He would hate, judge, or belittle himself, or me. Freedom! I now see God as kind and respectful.

What traits about God (or religion) do you dislike? How might you heal the roots of this negative aspect within yourself, so you may then experience a clearer vision of God?

New worldview

- I am loved and I am safe.
- God is so much more than the men in my life.
- God is the balance of all things: especially male and female traits.
- Spiritual people are just as human and frail as I. We all need compassion.

*"You can safely assume that you've
created God in your own image
if it turns out that your God hates
the same people you do"*
~ Anne Lamott

BALANCING EAST AND WEST

Either/or thinking may have you declare that God is either personal or universal. He is either male or female. He is real or
imagined. I'm sure you're certain about your conclusions. What
else is possible? The small, insignificant word "and" invites you
to explore the possibility that both seemingly opposite ideas
may be true! God is both personal and universal. God is both
male and female. God is both real and imagined. How can these
seeming opposites both be true?

Let's explore the idea that God is personal and universal.
Some scientists and philosophers have explored the idea that human beings are all connected and unified in a field of oneness.
Energetically, what affects one affects all. They say we are one
being on a cosmic level. This idea may indeed be true, yet we
can also know each other as individuals on very personal levels.
Since humans are both personal and universal, what if we open
to the experience that God is also personal and universal?

Both Eastern (generally universal) and Western (generally personal) philosophies are two sides of the same coin.

However, they are not complete when taken apart from one another. Both have aspects that are true, and exploring each of them may add to your wholeness and peace of mind. What if God (Love Itself) is both personal and universal—and—so much more than we can imagine and discover from this side of time? What if? How would this idea enrich your life?

SOME IDEAS TO EXPLORE ABOUT GOD:

1. The clearest viewfinder for the character of God is nature itself – that includes us humans.
2. Explore the natural world and you will find God revealed to you.
3. How will your life expand as you explore the idea that God is both personal and universal?
4. Breathe your way into experiencing the expanded ideas of God, and be still.
5. Those who embrace both aspects of God (personal and universal) get to experience the benefit, depth, and riches of this balance and wholeness. What will that look and feel like for you?

> *"God writes the Gospel not in the Bible alone,*
> *but also on trees, and in the flowers*
> *and clouds and stars."*
> ~ Martin Luther

GOD OR GODDESS?

God is the totality of being: a perfect combination of male and female. Since there is no pronoun for this combination, I will use He/Him/His throughout this book. God is both the masculine and feminine traits, *and* so much more. (In my next book I'll reference more of the feminine aspects of God.)

I invite the poets, writers and all those who love language to come up with a pronoun that signifies the combination of male/female. "Shim?" "Heesh?" Or my favorite: "Ze." Good wishes on this endeavor!

What about you? To what gender aspect do you most relate, at this time? What injuries have occurred in your life to influence whether you prefer God as male or female? Do you know that God is delighted no matter which aspect you follow? How much richer might your life be exploring God as Merciful Mother, Beloved Brother, Magical Wizard, or as Aslan?

You are loved and God will meet you where you are!

Feminine names for God: Love, Love Itself, Radiant One, Radiant Beloved, Holy One, Beloved Mother, Radiant Mother, My Beloved, Mother Most High, Merciful Mother, Beloved One…

Old worldview

- There is only one way to approach God.
- The only right way is the way I was taught. All other ways are wrong.

- I could go to hell for calling God by a different gender or name.

New worldview

- God is. What I have to say about the matter doesn't change anything.
- The Radiant One loves me and I'm safe in exploring all the ways she presents herself.
- I am loved and My Beloved will joyfully meet me on whatever path I take.

"GOD" IS NOT A NAME

God is a title like "Mr. President," or "Chairman," or "Father". The true names of our personal God have to do with how we relate to His character, nature, metaphoric qualities, and essence of being. "I am that I am," is how He introduces Himself in the sacred writings of the Hebrews and Christians.

HERE ARE OTHER NAMES BY WHICH GOD IS INTRODUCED:

- Adonai
- Jehovah
- Allah

- Brahma
- Shiva
- Gaia
- My Beloved
- Loving Papa / Mama
- Merciful Mother
- I am a rock, a solid foundation
- I am the bridegroom
- I am like a mother hen protecting her young
- She who brings into existence whatever exists

The list of the names of God is as endless as there are human beings; for even as a parent has different pet names for his children, we children have different names for our Father/Mother God.

For many reasons, some of us don't relate comfortably with a male deity. God, who fully understands the challenges of being human, meets us in whatever form will lead us closer to Love Itself. For instance, I had a client who was deeply religious, so in our session I was using the common name for God in her religion. The client stopped me and requested sheepishly if I'd mind calling God, *Aslan*, which is a fictional name for Jesus in the Chronicles of Narnia, by C.S. Lewis. The client made reference to experience with male violence as the reason for not feeling safe with the regular name for the male God. We proceeded with the session, and the client experienced profound love and freedom.

I invite you to explore the different aspects, genders, and names for God and find the name that connects you most deeply with Love Itself.

"More are the names of God and infinite are the forms
through which He may be approached.
In whatever name and form you worship Him,
through them you will realize Him."
~ Ramakrishna

God as Universal Source

There are many whose worldview does not have a comfortable place for a personal God. If this discomfort is currently true for you, embrace where you are and deeply explore God as the universal source of all that is. Here is an opportunity for another set of names that describe this universal aspect of God.

- Higher Power
- Creative Source
- Higher Self
- Divine Force
- All that is
- Universal consciousness
- Universal Father / Mother
- Universal Love

- Mother Earth
- Source of Life

In this book, I combine the personal and universal aspects of God and call Him/It: **Love Itself.** Love Itself works for me. Embrace the name for God that best suits you in this moment.

> *"Mother is the name for God*
> *on the lips and hearts of little children."*
> ~ William Makepeace Thackeray

THE HIGHER SELF

One worldview that can cause you to suffer is holding to the idea that you are alone in your life struggles. Sometimes angels and God may seem too high and remote. I propose that you're never alone and that your own higher self is always available to assist you.

What is the higher self? You could probably research the idea and find many different versions. I've found great comfort in the idea that only a portion of our soul energy inhabits this body during an incarnation. For fun, let's pretend that 65% of your soul stays on the other side in spirit form as the higher self and 35% comes into the body for this lifetime. We may, after all, only guess about such things. Let's explore how my higher self has been a great resource for help and healing.

THE HIGHER SELF HELPS WITH GRIEF:
My beloved dog Chewy was 14 years old, blind, deaf, and in pain. I kept asking that his angels take him home, yet he seemed determined to stay. I took him to a veterinarian who said, "The best gift you could give him is to put him to sleep." This declaration may have been true; however, I was emotionally unprepared for this next step. Under pressure from an authority figure, I made a hurried decision and agreed to let him go right then. I held him as they put the needle in, and he howled his last breath. To put it mildly, I became hysterical.

For eleven years, I cried and cried. I kept his howl a secret as I was so ashamed of causing him to suffer (my story). Eventually, I realized that I had new resources and tools for handling such grief, so I sat and called in my higher self to help me with healing this experience.

In a meditative state, I imagined going through the experience again. However, this time, I was aware that my higher self was in the corner waiting to assist. I had no idea what to expect and no plan for how to manage this healing. When I got to the portion where I'm holding Chewy, and they gave the shot, I saw his spirit leap from my arms into the embrace of my higher self. I saw and heard his joy, his wellness, his freedom from pain. He went from me to me (higher self) with great exuberance. As I watched this reunion transpire, I realized that he wasn't even in his body for the death howl, which had caused all my suffering. He was joyously free and had been all this time. Now I was free as well.

Here is another experience: My beloved mom died in her sleep when I was 30 years old and she was only 59. All of my brothers got to see her lying so peacefully "asleep" on the couch. I lived out of state and missed out on so much. Her death was, and is, the deepest pain I've ever felt in my bones. Yet, after the success with healing the passing of my fuzzy buddy, I wondered if this other great sorrow might also be healed.

I sat in a meditative state and imagined taking my whole self to the other side, into spirit form. I imagined sitting on the footstool, in front of my mom's sleeping body, waiting for her to pass and open her eyes on the other side. When she opened her eyes in spirit form, I was the first person she saw, and we had a delightful time as she realized that she was now at home in Heaven and that this earthly journey as Joan was finished. We laughed, hugged, and talked as we celebrated her life and our journey together. I also got to see her greeted by loved ones and make her way forward into the light, completely at peace. She was free, always had been, and now so was I.

A TRANSFORMATIVE EXPERIENCE WITH MY HIGHER SELF:
There was a part of me that was deeply exhausted by the difficult journey I had chosen for this life as Marie. I made arrangements to have a session with a coach who uses NLP (Neuro-Linguistic Programming) to work with the part of me that was tired. Deep in the process, we discovered that this part of me wanted to "go home" to the other side. It wasn't hurt, angry, or even sad, as it had worked through most of those challenges. This part of me

was, however, profoundly weary and longed for home and rest. Now, we NLP practitioners are trained to give the involved part what it wants and then integrate it back into the whole being. However, this part was not on board with that plan. So, the NLP coach asked for an internal wise part of me to come forward to facilitate the "going home" process, and what happened next stunned both of us.

I immediately saw my main guide for this life open up my energy field at the mid belly, and the weary part slipped past my guide, out of the opening, and was gone. There was deep stillness and silence in my body as my internal vision looked to the other side of my guide and saw my higher self waiting there. I heard a clear, "I'm ready" as he/she (higher self has no gender) entered and joined with this body. I felt my body jump, and I was filled to my fingers and toes with a larger, yet very familiar, energy. This energy being wasn't a stranger who had stepped into me. This was my higher self; that other portion of my soul that had been dwelling on the other side.

CHANGES I EXPERIENCED:

1. Everything was new: eating, sleeping, driving, people.
2. My voice was fuller and deeper. Friends near and far kept commenting on the change.
3. New clients asked who made my old hypnotherapy recordings as it "wasn't your voice."

4. There was a new feeling and presence of authority and trust.
5. Intuition took over my sessions, and I left formulas behind.
6. For a few weeks, I had difficulty using the right syntax when talking. I was confused when trying to tell stories from out there (spirit form) rather than in here (body).
7. I felt the need to reintroduce myself. However, I didn't because it would've been confusing to others. Instead, I'd greet their souls in the higher consciousness.

From the aforementioned experiences, you may see that the higher self is a great and ready resource for help, comfort, and healing. I invite you to explore, "What else is possible?" How might your higher self help you today?

> *"Your soul never incarnates completely.*
> *While you're in a body you also*
> *exist in higher dimensions."*
> ~ Annie Kagan

WHO IS GOD'S FAVORITE?

Since God is Love Itself and love is the heart of universal and unconditional affection, each and every one of us is His favorite! And yes, that means you *and* your worst "enemy" are His favorites! Your sports team and the opposing team; Americans and Mexicans; Christians and Muslims; and many more are His favorites! His personal love is more than big enough to embrace each one of us as His Beloved, and He is universal enough to know that there really is only one spirit. We are one and we are beloved.

Old worldview

- God has favorites.
- I'm in and my enemy is out.
- Muslims are in, Christians are out--or the other way around.
- God is in my heart.

New worldview

- "I am in the heart of God." ~ Kahlil Gibran
- Every single one of us is adored.
- EVERYONE: you, me, Hitler, your neighbor, that crazy person on the committee, etc.
- Their confusion is no worse than mine.
- I am the beloved and so are you.

"While I know myself as a creation of God,
I am also obligated to realize and remember that
everyone else and everything else
are also God's creation."
~ Maya Angelou

"My trust in God flows out of the
experience of his loving me,
day in and day out, whether the day is stormy or fair,
whether I'm sick or in good health,
whether I'm in a state of grace or disgrace.
He comes to me where I live and loves me as I am."
~ Brennan Manning

ONENESS

In my body there are many parts, each working for the unified goal of living in wellness. Each action and each reaction have the intent of creating a balance, so that life in this body may continue. I am a collection of many parts and yet I am one. So it is with all that exists. We are a collection of many sparks of being, yet also, we are one. Oneness is our true state of being; therefore, separation and aloneness are illusions we came here to dispel.

POSITIVE WORLDVIEWS:

- We are all connected on the cellular and spiritual levels.
- We can be personally known and also universally united with all that is.
- Oneness is our true state of being.
- Separation and aloneness are illusions.

- Aloneness is a state of mind and an illusion we are all here to face.
- What we do to others, we are also doing to ourselves.
- When we reject another person, we are in fact rejecting a part of our self.
- When one suffers, all suffer.
- When one expands his/her worldview and embraces love, we all benefit.
- When one person heals their wounds and opens their heart, we all benefit.

Affirmation: Every day, in healthy and creative ways, I embrace the common spark of life that lies at the heart of us all. I affirm the oneness of my human family. I allow and embrace differences and I wish for the peace, happiness, and well-being of all, for all, in all Love Itself. Blessed be our oneness.

"Everything and everyone is bound
together with some invisible strings.
Do not break anyone's heart; do not look
down on (those) weaker than you.
One's sorrow at the other side of the world
can make the entire world suffer;
one's happiness can make the entire world smile."
~ Shams Tabrizi

Who is Right about God?

Several citizens ran into a hot argument about God and different religions, and they could not agree upon a common answer. So they came to the Buddha to find out what exactly God looks like.

The Buddha asked his disciples to get a large elephant and four blind men. He then brought the blind men to the elephant and told them to find out what the elephant would "look" like.

The first blind men touched the elephant leg and reported that it "looked" like a pillar. The second blind man touched the elephant tummy and said that an elephant was a wall. The third blind man touched the elephant ear and said that it was a piece of cloth. The fourth blind man held on to the tail and described the elephant as a piece of rope. Each was certain of their own experience, so they got into a heated argument about the "appearance" of an elephant.

The Buddha asked the citizens: "Each blind man had touched the elephant, but each of them gives a different description of the animal. Which answer is right?"

The blind men are all correct; as are we from our current and limited points of view. We each experience God in our own unique way. In whatever way we see and experience God, as personal or universal, as Jewish or Hindu, Muslim or Christian, it is perfectly right for us in each moment of our life. Let us choose freedom for ourselves, and let us allow others to experience God as He presents Himself to them.

> *"You have brains in your head. You*
> *have feet in your shoes.*
> *You can steer yourself any direction you choose.*
> *You're on your own. And you know what you know.*
> *And YOU are the one who'll decide where to go..."*
> ~ Dr. Seuss

> *"When you feel a peaceful joy, that's*
> *when you are near truth."*
> ~ Rumi

JESUS IS THE DAO (WAY)
Jesus is the greatest master teacher (spiritual servant), and he came for each and every one of us. No one religion owns or may limit access to Jesus. His grace, mercy, wisdom, and love are already ours whatever path we choose. He shows us the way to Love Itself, and the grace he brings belongs to everyone. There is no opting in and converting is not necessary. He was not a Christian, nor does he require you to become one. In the religion of love, all belong without having to join. Stay where you are and be immersed in Love Itself, with Jesus as one of your guides.

Old worldview

- Jesus is exclusive to Christianity.
- One must say the sinner's prayer to have access to Jesus.
- If one doesn't resonate with that religious system, one must also reject Jesus.

New worldview

- Jesus belongs to all, without themhaving to join any religion.
- His loving grace, wisdom, and guidance belong to all.
- I can know Jesus as well as I know my best friend.

> *"Those who love me come from every system that exists...*
> *I have no desire to make them Christian,*
> *but I do want to join them in their transformation*
> *into sons and daughters of my Papa,*
> *into my brothers and sisters, into my Beloved."*
> ~ Wm. Paul Young

Spiritual Teachers

Jesus, Buddha, Quan Yin, Yogananda, and all other light-filled spiritual teachers come from the same Love. All light and love-filled truth comes from God and leads us back to God. These teachers are sign posts showing us the way to Love. Learn from them, love them, admire them, and keep moving forward. When you grab onto the admired sign post and declare this as the *only way* to God, you close to all other truth and limit your growth. When you cling to only one teacher and put him/her on a pedestal, you are bound to suffer eventually from a closed heart and judgment of others.

The temptation also exists to give your self-government over to the teacher or his representative (pastor, priest, imam, rabbi, etc.) Do not give away your power and authority to another. Be your own guru, keep your heart open to all that is true, and let love be the touchstone that keeps you on the right path for you.

Old worldview

- There is only one right way to God.
- I must find my pastor/priest/guru and follow him/her alone.
- I'm a mere mortal and will get easily lost.

New worldview

- Love is my touchstone for the journey.
- I only follow teachers and teachings inspired by Love Itself.
- Love leads me using many teachers.
- I maintain the spiritual authority for my life.
- All truth is God's truth.

"Buddha wasn't a Buddhist
Jesus wasn't a Christian
Mohammed wasn't a Muslim
Lao Tzu wasn't a Daoist
Nanak wasn't a Sikh
They were teachers who taught love.
Love was their religion."
~ Not sure who said it first.
Bless them!

Spiritual Messages

When I was living deep within conservative religion it was common to hear phrases such as: "God said _____." "He gave me this message for you _____." "This sacred text says _____." Sometimes, these messages were given to me in a way that didn't feel like love, it felt more like judgment and manipulation.

I am clear that God does indeed speak to us through sacred texts, books, and friends. I also believe He uses dreams, music, television, movies, astrology, tarot, runes and those perceived as enemies, to get our attention. The glorious and wild beauties of nature and the still small voice are among my favorite ways to hear from God. So, how does one know when it is God speaking, or when it's fear, or even manipulation?

CHECK EVERYTHING YOU THINK IS COMING FROM GOD:

- Does it feel like manipulation, judgment, or rob you of hope?
- Is someone trying to manage or control you for his/her sake or a group's benefit?
- Does the message make you fearful, or make your life feel smaller?
- Does the message make you feel excluded or shunned?
- Does it feel like the message got twisted by the speaker's fear-based worldview?

If yes, then NO! This is not love; therefore it is not from God.

- In contrast, does it make your life feel larger and liberated?
- Does your body respond with a surge of hope, relief, or joy?
- Is the message loving, kind, patient, and merciful?
- Does the message make you feel included, embraced, and celebrated?

If yes, then YES! This is love; therefore it is from Love Itself.

Be in your own relationship with God, and get your messages directly from Love. Be your own guru, pastor, or priest. You alone are in charge of your life, choices, and learning. Blaming a person or religious group for a wrong or unloving message (confusion) is a waste of time and energy, and it's inspired by fear. Consider it a learning opportunity, a wake-up call, and let go of your own confusion. Let Love be your yardstick for truth, for messages, and for forward movement. Love will reveal the right path for you.

All light and love-filled truth
comes from God and leads us back to God.
Ignore everything else.
~ Marie Maguire

"We all have a better guide in ourselves,
if we would attend to it,
than any other person can be."
~ Jane Austen

"There is a voice inside of you that whispers all day long,
'I feel that this is right for me, I
know that this is wrong.'
No teacher, preacher, parent, friend,
or wise man can decide
what's right for you — just listen to
the voice that speaks inside."
~ Shel Silverstein

WHO GOES TO HELL?

First off, if you're talking about other people, it's none of your business. Focus your energies on your own relationship with love and let love take care of everyone else. Second, when you opt out of spirituality or religion, does that mean you will go to hell? Nope. Hell is already present whenever you choose to live in fear with the sense of separation and aloneness, or choose to live with the feeling that you are not lovable or good enough. Not knowing you are loved is a form of hell that I don't wish on anyone! We each carry this sense of hell throughout our many lives until we are ready to release it, and have love and grace as a way of being. **Living loved is the road out of hell.**

What if you choose lifetime challenges that reject or dismiss spirituality or religion? What might you hope to experience or gain as a result of this chosen challenge? What if you live life after life in fear (hell) until you open your heart to Love Itself (heaven)? Might there be things you'll get to learn that cannot be embraced any other way?

I may trip and fall all along the way,
yet I will never be lost.
God knows where I am, and what I need,
and Love Itself is always there.
~ Marie Maguire

KARMA

MY UNDERSTANDING OF KARMA:
We hear that everything is energy, and scientists tell us that energy seeks its own balance. If the energy of your actions swings one way, it may swing the other way just as far. For instance, if in one life you move toward fear-based, power-seeking energy, you may someday experience the balance in the swing back.

Or maybe not!

> *"...the moment you forget what you have*
> *imagined or been taught karma to be,*
> *it becomes the moment you are spontaneously*
> *freed from the karmic wheel.*
> *This is the heart of liberation."*
> ~ Matt Kahn

KARMA AS ANOTHER WORLDVIEW:
Hell is one thought form for seeking justice and fairness in the world, Karma may be seen as another form. We humans seem to have a strong desire to feel that there is justice at some point and that punishment is on the way. Just like hell, karma seems to be another form of justice seeking. "They'll get theirs in this life or the next!" It may be a way of comforting ourselves, enjoying

revenge from a distance, or maybe even to keep us from carrying out our own version of revenge. I don't hear or feel love in any of those thoughts.

I don't feel love any time I hear about or study the karmic wheel.

What if our thoughts of right, wrong, and justice are wrong-side-out? What if we can't see, from our perspective, what is really happening here? What if our heartache and pain have another purpose in our life than what we're aware of thus far? If everything that comes to us comes through love first, might it help us to be curious and open-hearted as we explore the higher purpose and let go of the need for justice? Or fear of punishment?

For Heaven's sake, and with love's help, may we let go of the need for justice entirely. For, if we're all honest, and we're judging from a ground level perspective, none of us would survive the call for justice. We're all frail, foolish, and absurd. We've all done things from the state of confusion. The gifts that Jesus brings us are mercy and grace, so that we may forgive ourselves and others, and love as God loves us: whole heartedly, without reserve, with unfailing compassion, and with the tenderness of a mother's love.

So, if we let go of the need for justice and leave aside karma and hell, we may embrace the idea that our challenges are set in motion by our own preplanned goals for this life. If we are the planner of the challenges, and it isn't punishment or karma balancing, we may feel empowered to love what is and be curious about what it's producing in our souls.

I've worked with several healers and spiritual leaders whose numerology charts show them as highly developed souls, yet they experience extremely challenging lives. Often, they seem to have "tougher" lives than others. Instead of karma, these lives are about training, reminding, and developing compassion with the purpose of preparing them for their life's mission.

I've noticed that when well-meaning friends bring up karma as a reason for a present challenge, I experience negative reactions in my heart and body. When another friend brings loving awareness of the benefits of the challenge, I feel enlivened and hopeful. Love is a more empowering reason for everything we face.

Rather than karma balancing, what might your experiences be training you to be or to do?

Whatever challenge comes your way, it is an opportunity for fun and for learning. It's a chance to learn more about you and to find new ways of being in the world. Embrace it. Be curious. Live fully in this moment. Hold on, and go through the challenge with trust and faith that you are deeply loved and that all shall be well. You're not being punished. Be of good cheer!

Old worldview

- Difficult times are a sign of balancing karma.
- When you struggle, it's your own fault.
- You did something to deserve this _____.

New worldview

- Life is for fun and for learning.
- I am loved and all things come through love before they get to me.
- All challenges are an opportunity to grow.
- Indeed, they are an invitation to come higher in my understanding.
- At the very least, challenges can teach me compassion and empathy for others.

"The concept of an eye for an eye,
karmic equalizing of the score,
isn't the real deal.
Life is more of a learning thing."
~ Annie Kagan

"There is a brokenness out of which comes the unbroken,
a shatteredness out of which blooms the unshatterable.
There is a sorrow beyond grief which leads to joy
and a fragility out of whose depths emerges strength."
~ Rashani

God's love for me is huge and ever present.
He is my beloved and my source of peace!
~ Marie Maguire

What's up with Religion?

Most religions start out as a glorious, living spiritual movement with well meaning, free thinking, and radical (heretical) change. As more people gather as followers, a natural human attempt is made first to define, and then to regulate, the phenomenon. That definition includes rules and traditions about how to be in this particular community; all with the good intention to provide information, clarity, and structure. Soon, what was once an open and living organism for relationship with the Divine becomes entangled with rules, regulations, and fear. "If you claim to love God, and yet live, act, and/or believe differently than we do, one of us *has* to be wrong. Moreover, it cannot be us! Therefore, we must judge/fear/hate/shun/kill you to feel safe and right with our god or guru."

Religion in and of itself is a valuable resource for culture, learning, morality, and community. Alas, it is the fear-based thinking available in every style of religious (or human) organization that inspires un-loving actions and causes confused words and acts of violence.

Finding a Piece of the Truth – Zen Story

One day Mara, the Evil One, was traveling through the villages of India with his attendants. He saw a man doing walking meditation. The man's face was lit up with wonder. The man had just discovered something on the ground in front of him. Mara's attendant asked what that was, and Mara replied, "A piece of truth."

"Doesn't this bother you when someone finds a piece of truth, O Evil One?" his attendant asked. "No," Mara replied. "Right after this, they usually make a belief out of it."

An experience becomes a belief, a belief becomes a rule, and rules strangle the life out of spirituality and relationship with Love Itself.

Keep your religion, with all of its traditions and community, if you are so inspired, and see if you can let go of the rules and keep only love, Love, LOVE! **Be love, and live loved, within the tradition that inspires your heart.** Whenever you call upon God, wherever you feel inspired, every time you follow love, God will find you there.

Old worldview

- Religion is the only way to God.
- Rules are the right way to go. They make me right and you wrong.

New worldview

- The rule of love is all we need: Be kind, be respectful.

"Do not just read about generosity, BE GENEROUS.
Do not just talk about patience,
compassion, and unconditional love;
make them a part of your daily life!
It's not about being a Buddhist; it's
about being Buddha-like.
It's not about being a Christian; it's
about being Christ-like."
~ Timber Hawkeye

Fear-Based Religion (or Relationship)

Seriously, if you grew up within a religious system, how are you supposed to know if it's based in love or fear? All of your life you've been so close in that it may be a challenge to see clearly. Thankfully we can use relationships as an easy and safe representation to show what is healthy and what is not.

FEAR-BASED RELIGION IS LIKE HAVING A FRIEND OR PARTNER WHO DEMANDS:

- Call me every day. Calling me several times a day would be even better.
- Come see me in person at least three times every week.
- Wear certain kinds of clothes and even nicer ones in my presence.

- Watch your language everywhere, and especially watch it when you are near me and my other friends.
- Only read, think, and talk about what I say is acceptable.
- Behave in ways that are acceptable to the rest of my group of friends.
- Don't bring your messy life out into the open. Keep it to yourself. Pretend that everything is fine and that you are perfect.
- Know that every thought or question about the validity or form of our friendship is from The Enemy.
- Only associate with others who are friends with me the same way you are.
- Fear, hate, shun, or kill others who are not friends with me in this way.
- Fear my wrath for the slightest infraction.
- Feel guilt and shame whenever you even think you broke one of these rules.
- Feel great trepidation about losing my friendship.
- Be good because you are afraid of the consequences should you be otherwise.
- "Should," "ought," and "supposed to" must be your constant nagging companions.
- Fear is good because it keeps you safe here with me.

Whoa boy! Even writing these words makes me feel icky. You may not have had friends that were exactly like the one described above, yet you can imagine how scary and unloving it would be feeling trapped inside such a relationship. Society in general might think someone crazy to stay in relationship with friends, or lovers, who make these demands.

How does your religion stack up against the demands? Does your religion keep you connected by such fear-based tactics? If it does, then it's through confusion and a misunderstanding about love. Can you stay, yet rewrite new rules for yourself? What would you need to hear to give yourself permission to create a fear-free life? Or, a fear-free connection to your religion?

A reminder: Your beloved religious system did not set out to create a fear-based environment and, because it's so "normal," may not even realize how unloving it may have become. Be compassionate, merciful, and loving in your own movement toward Love Itself.

> *"Religion as a whole specializes in sin management.*
> *It's all about organizing humanity in such a way*
> *that we cause as little damage as possible."*
> ~ Erwin McManus

What Love Looks Like (with Spirit and Others)

Here we are with an opportunity to explore what real love looks like, and what it might ask of you. I invite you to let love sink into your heart and rearrange how you love yourself, others, and God.

LOVE IS LIKE HAVING A FRIEND, PARTNER, OR GOD SAYING:

- Whether we talk every day or twice a year, it feels as if we're never apart.
- I leave you free to be yourself; fully human with all your foibles.
- Bring your messy life out into the open and we will touch it gently.
- We laugh often and talk authentically.
- We are comfortable with silence.
- You read, think, and explore what interests you, trusting that love will be your guide.
- The more real you become, the more you feel whole, and the better our relationship becomes.
- You need to hide nothing, from yourself, others, or me.
- Everyone is your brother, and you love them as they are.
- Whatever Spirit guides you to do will ultimately enhance everyone's feelings of wholeness, happiness, and fulfillment, for love does no harm.
- Leave others free to be fully themselves, trusting them and their journey to Spirit's care.
- You let others follow Spirit as it seems right to them; relationships between friends are unique, after all.
- You naturally choose to hang out with others who are also kind, loving, and accepting.

- You embrace differences and learn from challenges.
- You feel peace, joy, and confidence that all is well.
- You know that you are safe.
- Fear is your main clue when you lose sight of love.
- Love is the glue that holds everything and everyone together.
- You are good to yourself and others because you love, and you wouldn't imagine being otherwise.

Prayer: I request a most benevolent outcome on my journey of releasing fear and all of its confusions. I trust love to guide me safely on my own unique spiritual journey. I choose to think, act, and speak from love, for wherever I bring or find love, there is God. I am part of Love Itself! Grant me the open heart that allows all others to follow Spirit in the way that seems right to them.

> *"God would prefer us all to be united than divided.*
> *The devil would prefer us all to be divided than united.*
> *God prefers the man who loves than the one who hates.*
> *The devil prefers the man who hates*
> *than the one who loves."*
> ~ Suzy Kassem

WHAT IS HERESY?

Heresy is a deviation or a difference of opinion from that which is presently accepted in a system of belief.

The label "heretic" is often used as a derogatory term and it's used to bully, to make people afraid, and to keep them in line with the currently accepted belief system (agreed upon world-view). It's a fear tactic that comes from man's attempt to keep other people in line and stay in power.

Famous heretics include the following people: Martin Luther, Galileo, Thomas Jefferson, Joan of Arc, Walt Whitman, King Solomon, King David, John Milton, Shakespeare, Michelangelo, Mark Twain, Mother Teresa, Saint Paul, Saint John, John Lennon, Socrates, Jesus, Buddha, and Abraham Lincoln. The list is truly endless.

I love all these "heretics" and I am honored if you count me among such wondrous company. God's love invites us to search, to question, and to explore our best path to Him and to Love Itself. May we all be heretics on the journey to living loved!

Old worldview

- Heresy is a bad thing.
- Being labeled a heretic is the worst.

New worldview

- Labeling another as a heretic is a form of oppression and violence.
- Love invites me to question and explore my relationship with God.

- I choose to be in the company (mentioned above) of such great souls!

"Heresy is another word for freedom of thought."
~ Graham Greene

*"The heresy of one age becomes the
orthodoxy of the next."*
~ Helen Keller

*"Don't be satisfied with stories, how
things have gone with others.
Unfold your own myth."*
~ Rumi

THE DARK NIGHT

Somewhere on this spiritual journey that we call life, in this or some other lifetime, you may experience a "dark night of the soul." It would be easy to interpret this dark night as depression, sadness, or prolonged grief. In the classic, pre-modern sense, it is not any of those things, and yet it may contain experiences of any, or all of, the aforementioned challenges. So, what is it? The deep dark of this spiritual night of the soul occurs when all that used to bring comfort and joy, all that felt like a connection to God, all that you held onto for hope, and all intimacy with the Beloved completely disappears. Moreover, it often feels like God is the one who cuts the cord of connection between you. Mine felt like a heavy curtain dropped between me and my Beloved. Words do not do justice to the feelings this inspired.

This darkness is by no means an hour, week, or month in duration. The experience usually lasts for many months, and sometimes it may even last for years.

There is a blessed purpose behind this darkness, and it is a gift that, at first, feels like a curse. It may feel as if you've lost your mind, your best friend, all hope, all connection, and all comfort. Yet, I assure you, it brings a beautiful gift. This darkness breaks open all certitude and judgment, opens your heart and mind, and calls you forward into a deeper relationship with God (and yourself) that transcends all religious structure.

This dark invitation into deeper relationship usually occurs because an individual says a prayer asking for a closer connection with God, "no matter what it takes." You are the one saying the prayer, but I believe it is said in response to an invitation by God, to come closer into authenticity and Love Itself.

How does one know if they have been in or through this dark night? Even if you don't define it the way I just did, it presents itself as a huge earthquake in one's life, and it's hard to miss. No other experience is quite like it. Since there is a sense of coming undone, like a caterpillar into a chrysalis, a desire for death is not uncommon. I've often wondered if there might be many more intuitive advisers/mystics/spiritual leaders among us if those who experienced spiritual emergencies (often labeled mental illness) were treated by those who understood the dark night and knew to give them the safe support and spiritual guidance they needed.

WHAT "THE DARK NIGHT" IS AND WHAT IT ISN'T:

- It is not caused by misfortune, tragedy or disappointment (as described by pop culture).
- It isn't being fed up with religion and throwing God overboard. That's another whole story!
- It may feel like God has suddenly thrown you overboard, and you don't know why.
- It may feel like you've lost your marbles and like God is moving far away from you.
- Prayer, scripture, meditation, and devotion dry up and blow away. **Nonetheless, you cling to God.**
- It is a deep spiritual transformation that looks and feels messy. However, it leads you closer to Love Itself.

> *"The dark night ... is nothing other*
> *than the story of a love affair;*
> *a romance between God and the human soul*
> *that liberates us to love one another."*
> ~ Gerald May, MD

EXAMPLES OF THE DARK NIGHT——MY STORY:
Jesus was an ever-present part of my life. Even before I understood religion, I saw His face in my mind and felt His love and closeness like a dear friend. Throughout the troubled times there was a sense of being supported, which made all the difference in my survival.

I confess I've been a bit of a rebel in this life. Raised Catholic (love the ceremony and mysticism), I became a conservative Christian (fellowship & music), yet, I was always questioning the rules and pushing boundaries. There seemed to be a divide between the love that I knew through Jesus and the dogma being taught. Yet, somehow, I muddled my way through church and tried to follow the rules. I wanted to be "right with God", be a good Christian girl, wife, mom, friend, and follower. The anxious pressure to be right with God led me to a fearful rigidness, an internal demand for perfection of myself and others, and an intensified lack of authenticity. Fear and authenticity don't play well together.

Years passed, and I went through my first divorce with the love and support that came with a close connection to God. Even though I struggled with fear, I was deeply aware of God's love and provision. Soon after the divorce, friends told me that I wasn't being authentic. Of course, I didn't really know how to be authentic, because I'd grown up in a frightening environment where I'd learned how to hide and pretend that all was well. You may imagine my greatest fear in becoming authentic was abandonment. I feared that I wouldn't be loved. Thankfully, my desire to heal and have complete wholeness was stronger than my fears, so I prayed, **"God, do whatever it takes to heal me and make me authentic in every way!"**

Whoosh!! A thick dark curtain fell and completely cut me off from Jesus. And, just as I had feared, those friends abandoned me as well. Devastation, confusion, oh yes! Yet, Jesus soon started speaking to me in new ways, including dreams and visions, which helped me understand this time of darkness as a good thing. I found books to comfort me and spiritual quotes that enlivened me. Compassionate friends stepped in to love and help. Amazing support happened all along the twenty plus years.

I can't do my transformational journey justice here; so, let me say that the dark night took me from fear to love, and from hiding to authenticity. Every act of confusion taught me well what I needed to know. Through the many years of darkness **I learned to hold on to faith and to trust in love. I came to know God beyond the structure of religion.** Even though I've moved beyond religion, I honor its place and value in the journey. Living in the light, my heart is open, and I'm equipped to love myself and my neighbors and embrace the mystery that is Love Itself.

"Not all those who wander are lost"
~ JRR Tolkien

"When the light comes on you'll find

that you've gotten rid of everything
that was afraid to be alive."
~ Unknown

ANOTHER DARK NIGHT SHARED BY A FRIEND, IN HER OWN WORDS:

"The dark night of the soul interrupted my quiet life like a sudden, violent storm. I had been a deeply spiritual person for 20 years. I lived my Christian faith wholeheartedly in everything I did, from Bible studies to being a youth pastor and from prayer meetings to the prayer closet. Yet, a prayer rose up within me one day, **asking God to do whatever it took to take me deeper into Him**. *Three months later, in the middle of the night, a single thought arose, "What if there is no God?" It appeared like a thief, threatening to take away all of my faith. What I didn't know then, that I discovered in the months of fear and torment that followed, was that my faith was being refined in the furnace of the dark night of the soul. Like silver, all the impurities were being skimmed off the top; something I never could have done on my own.*

"I began to ask myself the BIG questions: "Who is God?" and "What is love?" Perhaps most importantly, I asked, "Who am I?" I had to assume I didn't know anything, because as it turns out, I don't. It was the most terrifying and deeply transforming experience of my life. Going from thinking I knew everything to not knowing anything was very disorienting. I felt like I was losing my mind. I was taken deeper into God, but it wasn't at all what I thought it would be. Like Alice through the looking glass, I entered a world that was more expansive, more incredible, more mysterious than I could ever have imagined. That is the beauty

*of these dangerous kinds of prayers; we can never experience any-
thing other than our own limited understanding without Divine
intervention. God blew my mind. And this is the wild kind of
living faith I'm learning to dwell in now, without boundaries,
without fear, without knowing.*

*"My walk with God looks very different now. I don't do Bible
studies, though my shelves are filled with teachings from many
perspectives, including the Bible. I'm no longer a youth pastor.
I don't go to prayer meetings or to the prayer closet, though I
do find myself communing continuously with God, especially in
nature, with love and gratitude for all there is. I still ask myself
the big questions. I just don't expect an answer. That way, the
question keeps taking me deeper into the unknown and into the
mystery that is God."*
~ Julie Calvez Stinson

Life is a grand adventure or nothing at all!
~ Helen Keller

WHAT DOES ONE DO IN THE MIDST OF THIS, OR ANY, KIND OF
DARKNESS?

1. God (Love Itself) is your guide, so you can know that you
are secure even in the darkness. Tell yourself, and keep
telling yourself, that this time of darkness is a gift that
leads to great joy.
2. Old familiar habits will not lead you to this new and expanded destination. Seek out help, comfort, and support
from spiritual companions who truly understand.

a. I am one of those who would be honored to walk with you. I live, love, and teach from a borderless spirituality.

b. The Catholic Church has religious sects that are good at understanding and supporting those in the dark night of the soul. They also have spiritual direction opportunities available.

c. Sufi's are the mystical sect of Islam and may offer support for this inner journey.

3. Read many books or watch YouTube videos on every topic that draws you.

4. Know that Love Itself will send you people, books, songs, and dreams that will guide you safely.

5. If at all possible, find a friend who has been through or is currently in the dark night as well. Walk together!

a. Expect that your journeys will be unique, yet similar.

b. Be very kind, patient, and loving toward each other.

c. Learn and use non-violent communication.

6. Keep journals of your experience, especially documenting the comfort God sends your way.

7. **Take no action inspired by fear.** Also, do not listen to the faint hearted naysayers.

8. Cling to God (not church or religion) with the zeal of Job 13:5, "Though he slays me, yet will I wait for him: nevertheless, I will maintain my ways (of faith) before him."

9. **Do not be afraid, for you are loved! Hold firm to inspired words that comfort you.**

10. The darkness may last months or years, but no matter the length, the dawn will arrive at the right moment, with

great freedom, gratitude for every moment, and joy in living loved.

"New beginnings are often disguised as painful endings."
~Lao Tzu

Throughout time, it has been the mystics who have talked about this dark night of the soul, and many good books have been written on the subject if you would like to know more. See a few reading recommendations in the Reference Section of this book.

"Times of great calamity and confusion
have been productive
for the greatest minds.
The purest ore is produced from the hottest furnace.
The brightest thunder-bolt is elicited
from the darkest storm."
~ Charles Caleb Colton

CHUCKING GOD OVERBOARD

The dark night is when it seems that God has thrown us overboard. Yet, it turns out to be an invitation to greater connection. So, what happens when one gets fed up with religion and *you* are the one to throw the whole thing out, God and all? I've met many people who've done it. Most didn't realize at the time that God and religion are two separate things.

HERE IS A RANGE OF ATTITUDES I'VE SEEN IN THOSE WHO'VE THROWN OUT "GOD."
EACH STEP MAY TAKE YEARS OR MANY LIFETIMES!

- Anger and resentment toward religion, and thus toward a personal God
- Outspoken desire to abolish all religious systems
- Judgment of those who are foolish enough to still be religious
- "I'll do it myself," atheistic leanings
- Repeatedly falling down and realization of need for help
- Openness toward a non-personal God such as Universal Source or Higher Power
- Life gets better, yet something is still missing
- Acceptance of possibility of a personal God
- Eventual disconnecting a personal God from religion
- Curiosity about the journey, and the valuing of relationship with God
- Forgiveness for all that came before
- Acceptance and honor for the value of religion
- Embracing the balance of a personal and universal God
- Leaving everyone free to follow their own inner guide

Wherever you are on that continuum is just right for you, right now. It wouldn't surprise me if we all spent lifetimes exploring life beyond any religious or spiritual belief system. What might be gained? If it's all for fun and for learning, could you ever really go outside the safety and embrace of Love Itself? Does that

Love allow you to search, to question, and to explore? If your current worldview says, "yes" then part of you is already living loved.

> *"Keep me away from the wisdom which does not cry,*
> *the philosophy which does not laugh*
> *and the greatness which does not bow before children."*
> ~ Khalil Gibran

FEAR OF GOD: GETTING CLEAR ABOUT SEMANTICS

Having a "fear of God" can mean the following: being respectful, reverent, worshipful, deferential, and courteous (in a playful, loving, and joyous way). I find all of these words helpful in exploring who God is in my life.

Fear of God can also mean the following: being fearful, scared, terrified, worried, anxious, timid, or feeling like a worthless worm. None of these mix well with what I know of Love Itself.

When you let love be the guidepost leading you safely to God, embrace the first list and completely let go of the second. You will be glad you did. Fear and worry always leads to confusion. Love, reverence, deference, and joy—each of these keeps you safe within Love Itself.

Old worldview

- God is scary
- I am a worthless worm

New worldview

- God is Love Itself
- I am safe within that love
- I am the beloved child of Love Itself
- Joy invites me into a warm embrace

"There is no fear in love.
But perfect love drives out fear,
because fear has to do with punishment.
The one who fears is not made perfect (complete) in love."
~ 1 John 4:18, NIV

Brain Dominance and Spirituality

It has been my observation that those who are primarily left-brain dominant seem less inclined to be open to, interested in, or in the practice of exploring spiritual themes. Yet, they may find cultural value in participating in a defined religious structure. When they do explore spiritual topics, they are scientifically thorough in their research and desiring of certitude. They want to find the right, true, and real God, where clear boundaries and checklists of behavior can make them feel safe and virtuous. They mostly rely on research, proof, and right thinking.

People who are mostly right-brain dominant are more likely to explore and be interested in a broad spectrum of spiritual matters, which may include religion, spirituality, energy healing, intuition, psychic phenomena, astrology, tarot, runes, etc. There is less call for certitude, and more openness to not knowing all the details or having definitive proof. They often rely on experience, intuition, and right feelings.

Is brain-dominance fixed and unchangeable? There is a flexibility of focus that I invite you to explore. For example, when I was working as an executive, my mind was focused on linear, analytical, and organizational functioning. During that time, I had difficulty painting or doing other creative activities, and my spirituality was more habitual. Now that my job is more right-brained and creative, I paint, write, and explore a broader spectrum of spirituality. Admittedly, I have easy access to both sides of my mind, and there are many who seem to have a primary dominance. Still, with recognized value, clear intent, willingness, and persistence, I believe it is possible to expand pathways to the right side of the mind that more easily experiences God, spirituality, peace, creativity, oneness, imagination, empathy, etc.

So, what happens if your interest in God, religion, and spirituality is a matter of biology and hemispheric functions? What if your dominant brain hemisphere is part of your plan for this life, including its gifts and challenges? Would Love Itself judge or condemn someone for having a brain, in this lifetime, which was not inclined to be open toward spirituality or personal relationship with God? What if, over many lifetimes, you experience and explore God from both sides of the mind? Might there be some fun and value in exploring life from these different perspectives?

For a bit of fun, I invite our left-brained brothers and sisters to step to the right side of the mind, and explore "What else is possible?"

Old worldview

- My way of thinking and being is the only right way.
- Who I am is fixed and unchangeable.

New worldview

- Both right and left brain thinking are a valid way to experience the world.
- Balance is always a good idea.
- My way is right for me and your way is right for you.
- It is all for fun and for learning.

> *"Based upon my experience with*
> *losing my left mind (stroke),*

I whole-heartedly believe that the
feeling of deep inner peace
is neurological circuitry located in our right brain."
~ Jill Bolte Taylor

ANGELS, GUIDES, AND ANCESTORS

Whether you believe in and connect with angels, guides, and ancestors, or prefer leprechauns, elves, and fairies, or prefer to limit yourself to only having connection with God the Father, you get to decide the best path to explore the sacred. We are all unique. We are all beloved, and Love Itself approaches us and draws us home in our own distinctive way.

Let us ease up on ourselves and each other and drop the judgments. Allow fun, joy, and companionship to lead you on to a greater connection with all that is. If love leads you to explore and enjoy the support of these helpers, then celebrate. Or, if it suits you better, completely ignore these resources and trust Spirit to lead you your own way. Arguing validity does not lead to love, respect, or connection. So my friends, **to each his own unique journey, with love and respect**.

"Those who don't believe in magic will never find it."
~ Roald Dahl

"The person with an experience
is never at the mercy of a person with an argument."
~ Unknown

"I believe in everything until it's disproved.
So I believe in fairies, the myths, dragons.
It all exists, even if it's in your mind.
Who's to say that dreams and nightmares
aren't as real as the here and now?"
~ John Lennon

CONTRADICTIONS

An expanded worldview eventually asks us to be at peace with the mystery of contradictions, of holding both sides as possibly true. This openness creates the opportunity to hold seemingly opposing beliefs in respectful balance, such as the idea that God is both personal and universal at the same time.

Other contradictions may be that karma exists, yet it doesn't. We are all separate, yet one. We can all follow Love Itself, yet do it in completely different ways. Time feels linear, yet there is only ever NOW. You can know the way to God, yet really know nothing at all.

Some can embrace the mystery of contradiction sooner and easier than others. We will all do it at the moment that is right for our journey. Take a deep breath and be at peace, Beautiful Soul, for all is well.

"I don't know," is a wise statement.
~ Marie Maguire

"If anyone thinks they know something,
they don't yet know as much as they should know."
~ Corinthians 8:2, CEB

Judging Right and Wrong

Right and Wrong – Zen Story

When Bankei held his weeks of meditation, pupils from many parts of Japan attended. During one of these gatherings, a pupil was caught stealing. The matter was reported to Bankei, along with the request that the culprit be expelled. Bankei ignored the case.

Later, the pupil was caught in a similar act, and again Bankei disregarded the matter. This angered the other pupils. They drew up a petition asking for the dismissal of the thief, stating that otherwise they would leave in a body.

When Bankei had read the petition, he called everyone before him. "You are wise brothers," he told them. "You know what is right and what is not right. You may go somewhere else to study if you wish, but this poor brother does not even know right from wrong. Who will teach him if I do not? I am going to keep him here even if all the rest of you leave."

A torrent of tears cleansed the face of the brother who had stolen. All desire to steal had vanished.

All wrong-doing comes from a confused attempt to get love.

Any and every time one of us does something foolish or violent, it is a desperate attempt to get the love we crave. Some say we need love even more than food. Children have even died who had plenty of food and no love. It's called a failure to thrive. Even as adults we can fail to thrive in our life because we don't know how to get the love we need. Love may seem so inaccessible that we reach for power instead.

In our desperation we become confused and fill that space with other things that may range from slightly to thoroughly off-kilter. Examples going from slight to extreme are around us every day: codependency, overeating, all manner of addictions, bullying, theft, verbal and physical violence, suicide and murder.

Shunning or punishment will not put the confused person on the right track to better behavior. How might the world be different when we truly understand such confusion, respond with compassion, and create ways to put people on the right track to Love Itself? Of course, many of those who are dangerously confused may need to be detained until their minds and hearts are set on the right track.

In my own life experience, I've done many confused things in repeated attempts to get the love (safety, security, belonging, etc.) that I craved. I did those things again and again until it got through to me that they didn't get me where I wanted to go, so I stopped. I cried out for help and wisdom. The road away from confusion felt long and hard, yet since then I've been faced with similar choices and have made very different decisions. I'm no longer confused.

My experience with confusion has taught me mercy and compassion. It has given me the opportunity to work through fear and shame. It was a perfect set up to become who I am today.

Where have you been confused? What foolish things have you done in an effort to calm down the misery of that confusion? What will your life be like when you cease judging yourself and others about confused attempts to get love? How at present can you give mercy and love where it's needed?

An astrologer was reading my birthchart and exclaimed in astonishment; "You will do many foolish things in this life with the intent to become gentle and merciful. If you didn't do these things you would have been an arrogant and impatient spiritual teacher. You would have harmed others." This information came years after the confusion ended and was confirmation that, not only had I planned this life, I was on the right track every step of the way.

All wrong-doing, all sin, all illegal activities, all abuse, all terrorist actions, all foolishness comes from a confused attempt to get love. Period. The only way to end these things is to help people cease to be confused, which may also include making sure that they have food, shelter, medical help, education, meaningful work and community connections/family. Without such basic needs being met we all become desperately confused.

Old worldview

- All wrong-doing is sin
- Wrong doers are evil.

New worldview

- All wrong-doing is a confused attempt to get the love we need.
- Wrong doers are confused and need compassionate help.
- We have all been confused, therefore we all need compassion.

"Never be ashamed! There's some
who'll hold it against you,
but they're not worth bothering with."
~ J. K. Rowling

There are no mistakes, only opportunities to learn.
Regrets are a waste of time and energy,
and are inspired by fear.
Make amends when possible, or pay
it forward, and move on.
~ Marie Maguire

Nonviolent Communication

It is my desire to spread the news about nonviolent communication (NVC). I'm a novice at it; nevertheless, I've already seen and experienced its value at creating peace and connection between people.

Our everyday language is violent when we label, compare, demand, diagnose, and utter judgments on our self or others. When our needs aren't met, we seem to be accustomed to thinking about and pronouncing what we think is wrong with people. Some of us might shut down, sulk, and expect the other person to magically know what's wrong, and get mad when they don't. Most of us are not so good at expressing our emotions, or asking directly for what we need. Instead, we make verbally violent declarations that arouse equally violent reactions, and then, unsurprisingly, nobody gets what they need.

People who are verbally violent are often ordinary human beings who are in pain, and in need of compassion! In fact, if we're honest, that's all of us. We are each verbally violent until we become conscious of the violence, learn new ways to express our feelings, and ask for our needs to be met.

> *"What others say and do may be the stimulus,*
> *yet it is never the cause of our feelings.*
> *Our feelings result from how we choose to think about*
> *what others say and do."*
> ~ Marshall Rosenberg, PhD

HERE ARE A FEW EVERYDAY EXAMPLES OF VIOLENT COMMUNICATION:

- I think you should…
- That's nothing; wait till you hear…
- Cheer up. Don't feel so bad.
- How could you let this _____ happen?
- What's wrong with you?
- You are such a (narcissist, cry baby, know-it-all…)
- You're only looking for excuses.
- You are too (sensitive, slow, smart…)
- Why don't you smile more?
- Are you really going to wear that?
- Why? (This word, all by itself, can inspire defensiveness.)

I remember the moment when I woke up to the reality of violent communication by normal, decent human beings. Many years ago, I watched Maya Angelou speaking on the Oprah Winfrey show. She talked about relationships and pecking ducks. Ms.

Angelou said something about how some people "don't have the nerve to reach up and grab your throat, so they take little pieces of you with their rude comments." It's like they are taking bites out of your soul (pecking ducks), and we don't have to allow those bites. The sun shone, the sea parted, and I was on dry ground for the first time in my life.

I grew up around violent communication, I've used it, and I've watched it on television. Now, I was invited into a world where language was nonviolent, kind, and more effective at getting needs met.

NON-VIOLENT COMMUNICATION LEAD-IN IDEAS:

1. What do you need right now? How may I support you in meeting that need?
2. When (this) happens, I feel (angry, scared, sad), because I need (yep, you've got to say your need aloud). Therefore, I would like to (proposed action).
3. When I hear you say those words in that way, I feel scared. I need more safety in our conversation.
4. I sense that you're feeling afraid. Is that how you feel?
5. I'm grateful to you for telling me what you heard. I realize that I didn't make myself as clear as I'd have liked, so let me try again.
6. I'm exhausted and I really don't have the energy to deal with the noise of the music. I want some peace and quiet (expressing need/no fault finding)!

Example: One day I was in conversation with a dear friend and I heard her say something that poked one of my deep fears. Without a moment's forethought, I responded with angry words. She quietly said, "I wonder if you are feeling afraid?" I burst into tears and we had a conversation that deepened our relationship rather than ending it. Her nonviolence changed me and inspired my desire to know more about this great resource.

For more information go to http://www.nonviolentcommunication.com/ and read Marshall B. Rosenberg, PhD, Nonviolent Communication: A Language of Life.

Old worldview

- The only kind of violence is physical violence.
- I am a victim of how others respond to me.

New worldview

- Verbal violence is just as destructive as physical violence.
- I'm responsible for how I say things. I choose to learn nonviolent communication.
- World peace begins with me. How I say things makes my world peaceful or violent.

"Raise your words, not your voice.
It is rain that grows flowers, not thunder."
~ Rumi

WHAT IF WE LIVE MORE THAN ONCE?

There was a time in my life, in my worldview, when the idea of living life after life was the worst form of hell I could imagine. And I said so at every opportunity. In my mind, this life was so difficult and painful that I would never, ever, ever want to come back here again. Ever. Then my worldview began to expand in ways such that, eventually, I had to consider this idea of reincarnation as a possibility. I read books, asked open and honest questions, studied past-life hypnotherapy, and unwrapped my curiosity. What I discovered blew open my worldview, healed my wounds, and even became a treasured resource for embracing Love Itself.

WHAT IF . . .

- We have lived many lifetimes?
- We have explored different challenges?
- We have been male and female, Hebrew and Greek, black and white?
- We have had many partners, children, parents, "enemies"?
- It's all for fun, and for learning?
- This lifetime as (insert your name) is another opportunity to learn, grow, and have fun?

What if? Sit with each possibility for an hour or a month. Let it soak into your heart and open the doors to, "What else is possible?" What peace might be found? What suffering might be released? What other facet of your self is available? How might you embrace and collect every bit of yourself? What compassion and forgiveness could be found within this idea? What grief might be relieved? What adventures are left to be explored?

For example: Maybe in this life you deeply desired to have children, yet weren't able? Certainly this desire and felt limitation would bring opportunities to grow. The pain of longing might be eased by embracing the idea of living other lives. You may have had children many times before, and may again in future lives. For whatever reason, you might have desired to explore the challenges of a childless lifetime. Might this new worldview bring some ease to the pain and a sense of adventure for exploring other possibilities this time around?

> "...Then you would get more and more adventurous
> and you would make further and further out
> gambles (of) what you would dream.
> And finally, you would dream where you are now.
> You would dream the dream of living the
> life that you are actually living today."
> ~ Alan Watts

A FEW OF MY PAST LIVES:
I share these with the view of showing how knowing and healing your past lives might heal and enhance your life this time around. Every time I helped and healed those earlier parts of me, I gained the benefits. If you find this information laborious then skip on to the next section.

As a very large young man in early times, I was being led by the tribal village out into the barren land far away from home. I was mentally simple and becoming a dangerous problem for everyone because I was physically hurting people without understanding what I was doing. Out of love and survival necessity, I was being taken out to die. They took most of my fur clothing and told me to stay. I did, thinking this was a game. Eventually, I froze to death in great wailing confusion.

My current self went back and stayed with him, gently cradling and caressing this child man until he passed. This time, he wasn't alone.

A man in early times, I had been out hunting, and when I came back to the cave, it was empty. I was simple enough that I stood there in abject confusion. I felt abandoned and bewildered.

My current self went back to him, as if in a vision, and put my hands on his chest to give him some of my current knowledge and resources. I felt his aching physical pains and also saw his eyes light up with more awareness and understanding. He felt empowered and now knew what to do to find his people.

A short man in a grass hut village, I was good, gullible, and easily convinced by the powers that be that I needed to do a really dreadful thing that would help my village. When my wife and I killed our beloved daughter, as commanded, the village medicine man turned everyone against us. We discovered too late that he did this manipulation to gain more power. We were tied to grass mats, mud was put on our eyes, and we were floated out into the stream to slowly drown.

My current self met the short gullible man in the inter-life (between lives), helped him understand what happened, updated his internal resources, and took him back into that life so he could catch this Power Hungry Fellow in his own trap. They pretended to kill their daughter, and when they came to report their action, others were in hiding to hear what was said. The Power Hungry Fellow lost everything and was banished. The old me gained standing in the village, and I felt empowered to live honorably. Unexpectedly, the current me lost all fear of dark water.

As a male priest in ancient Egypt I led an honored and peaceful life. No healing needed. I access the energy of this life when I need more peace of mind.

As a young girl in Israel I was running the dusty streets and playing with my friends, when I came upon a group of people gathered around someone. I wiggled my way in to see what was happening and saw it was only a man talking. I turned to go. However, this man was so different, not in looks, but in presence. I stayed and watched. He called me to sit beside him, and I watched him. I have no idea what he said, yet I was captivated. When he was finished speaking and was getting ready to go, he picked up my hands, looked deep into my soul, and kissed them. My hands became enflamed with an internal fire, and I somehow knew I had been called to service. I saw him several times and became one of the pesky children who followed him.

His face has been in my mind since that time. In all of this life, He has been one breath away from my awareness. As a child, when I'd watch movies of His life, I would rail against them saying, "He didn't look like that. He didn't talk like that. He didn't act like that." He is an ever present part of my journey. One of my next books may be about this man that I know: Yeshua/Rabbi/Jesus

As a female healer in the dark ages, who lived on the edge of society, I provided valued services. Eventually, societal fears caused me to be hunted with the intent to kill me as a witch. I took my own life rather than submit to their judgment.

My current self met her in the inter-life (between lives), and gave her a clearer understanding of how things work. She felt so much better. She chose to reenter that life long before anything bad had happened. With this new understanding, she prepared safe caves to hide in for when the time came. She lived with far more peace and joy and found the process fun rather than scary. She still took her own life in the end, yet it came from a more empowered and peaceful place. "That was fun," were her first words upon reentering the inter-life.

As a male First People's shaman, I led a peaceful life in the Pacific Northwest before white incursion.

As a male Catholic priest, I was from a wealthy family, yet I chose to live a life of service and teaching. My current self went back and asked him to lay down his vows at the end of that life, so that I could have greater freedom in this life. We had a delightful walk and chat.

As the wife of a slave owner in the Deep South, my husband fathered several children from the slave women on our plantation. One was a boy who was light enough to pass in white society, so I taught him to read, prepared him to live as a white man, and helped him escape to freedom in the West.

As a male born into a mob family, I knew I wasn't mob material, and yet I was afraid of my mother, and out of that fear, I did not break away to become my real self. They shipped me off to Las Vegas to be a low-level business man mobster.

My current self met this past-self man in the inter-life and helped to upgrade his understanding with what I know now. He felt empowered, decided to go back into his early life, and made brand new decisions. He was successful in communicating his desired life with his mom and priest. With their combined support, this time, he chose a life of creativity and service.

Old worldview

- I live only once.
- This life is my only chance to do and get everything I want.

New worldview

- I have and will live many lifetimes.
- I get to explore life from many perspectives: male/female, rich/poor, parent/childless, etc.
- I will experience many types of partners, children, challenges, etc.
- When I heal past lives I'm also healing myself in this life.
- It's all for fun and for learning.

> *Every time we empower and heal our past lives,*
> *we heal and empower ourselves. It is that simple.*
> ~ Marie Maguire

WHAT IF WE PLAN OUR LIVES?

Many people embrace the idea that we are eternal beings. You may have considered the possibility that the essence of your soul comes here repeatedly and is the same from life to life to life. Whether you believe that or not, I invite you to meditate on the possibility that you may have fully participated in the planning of the upcoming life as (insert your name).

Imagine the planning session, including all who would be involved. Many possibilities lie before you! For whatever reason, you chose this life you are now living. Your goals influence and set in motion the life ahead. Your purpose influences the layers of challenges you'll face: gender, race, ethnicity, personality and temperament, strengths and weaknesses, parents, and family structure, to name a few.

No matter what you are presented with in this life, it is all for fun and learning. Everything and everyone are a gift to help you reach your intended goals.

IF YOU PLANNED THIS LIFE AS (INSERT YOUR NAME):

1. Every challenge you face is a perfect set-up to learn and grow.
2. What gifts are those challenges trying to give you?
3. Discover what you got to learn from your parents, both from who they were and who they weren't.
4. Be curious about what you had to learn on your own because of the challenges your parents faced.
5. How have physical challenges influenced your life decisions and options?
6. What are you passionate about? Your passion may be a clue as to what you are here to accomplish.

One of my main challenges was communication. I set up many opportunities for my voice to be stifled. All for the purpose of learning how to, and how not to, communicate. Since communication was my challenge it is also one of the gifts I bring to this world.

My passion is for all things spiritual. I've read countless books, explored many traditions, and it is my preferred topic of conversation. This passion is what I'm here to bring the world using my communication challenge!

I invite you to explore this idea for yourself. What are your challenges? What are your passionate interests? And how might they combine to lead you to your heart's desire for this life?

Old worldview

- Life just happens.
- I'm a victim of how things turned out.

New worldview

- I was an active partner in the planning process for this life.
- I chose the challenges and opportunities that I'd face.
- Everything and everyone are a gift to help me reach my intended goals.

> *"More learning can occur when there are many obstacles*
> *then when there are few or none.*
> *A life with difficult relationships,*
> *filled with obstacles and losses,*
> *presents the most opportunity for the soul's growth."*
> ~ Brian L. Weiss

WHO AM I?

Who am I? How you answer this question reveals the layered stories of the role you are playing in this lifetime. Your answer also reveals the perspective from which you are seeing yourself at this moment.

From deep within the dream of this life, I would describe myself as a female of Irish descent, only girl among five brothers, an elf in a hobbit's body, a socialized hermit who loves to read, an artist, an author, and one who has survived a traumatic childhood. Obviously, much more could be said.

From a higher perspective, I'd say I am a soul who is playing the role of Marie Maguire. I am so much more than this body, gender, and temperament. I am one with all that is and deeply loved by the Beloved. I'm here to help people connect to love and live free of fear. I chose a life story that would give me the opportunity to explore fear and love because they helped develop the gifts I'm here to bring this time around.

We are eternal souls dwelling in a body for a short time. Since we come here again and again, we have been other genders, other personalities, other races. Really allow the deep, quiet inner self to explore and feel the variables of this possibility. We are not this personality, gender, temperament, color, or race. The story labels are fun for awhile, for they are the lenses and challenges that we chose to live in and learn from in this life. I'm curious what life will be like when we become playful, let go of attachment to labels, and live from our eternal soul that is so much more. We are not our labels, and neither is anyone else.

Who am I? Answer this question for yourself, again and again, from both ground level and higher perspectives. Meditate on what life will be like free of the labels and stories. Expand your worldview any time your labels or stories cause you to suffer.

> *"Religion survives because it answers three questions*
> *that every reflective person must ask.*
> *Who am I? Why am I here? How then shall I live?"*
> *~ Jonathan Sacks*

Our Stories about Others

All of our stories, and our interpretations of others' stories, are about our own suffering and worldview. No matter what we think about someone, our internal stories are really all about who we are. We alone are responsible. What others do, say, or believe, even if aimed at us, has nothing to do with us. Their opinions are all about what is going on inside of them and the content of their worldview. Nothing is personal.

Deal with and heal yourself first, last, and in-between. Learning to question your thoughts is a big leap toward peace of mind. When you question your internal stories, you can love yourself, give yourself what you need, take empowered action, communicate in a clear, loving and nonviolent fashion, and stop crucifying others for being different. What might the world be like? When you have peace, the world will have more peace.

Old worldview

- My interpretation of other people's words and actions is accurate.
- I can believe all of my thoughts.
- Even if the other tells me they didn't mean it the way I interpreted it, I'm always right.
- What others say about me is true.

New worldview

- I see the world through the filter of my worldview.
- My interpretation is blurred by my own beliefs.
- When I react based on my distorted interpretation, I and those around me will suffer.
- I need to do inquiry to get clear about what is true and what is untrue.
- Only then do I see clearly enough to take empowered action.
- What others say about me is based on their worldview and it's all about them.

Eccentricity is a matter of perspective;
to some I am conservative

others find me loony
another may be enthralled,
and call me deep Mother hugs.

I've come to know that whatever you see
comes honestly
through the filter of your own confusions.
I choose to live free,
and live and love and dance radiantly.
~ Marie Maguire

WE ARE NOT OUR THOUGHTS

Around the age of six or seven, when we begin to wonder if there really is a tooth fairy (or any other regionally correct childhood belief), the critical factor is being formed in our physical mind. When this process occurs it creates a division between the conscious and subconscious mind. This process also creates the voice that you hear talking inside your head. That voice is part of the physical body; it is not you. You are the eternal soul who lives in the body and hears the voice. When you pass on from this life, that internal voice stays and dies with the physical body.

This voice is a part of the physical mind and its main purpose is survival. It loves to search out problems and chew on them until it comes up with a solution. That's its job. The trouble that arises is that it never runs out of problems to chew on, so there is constant fear-based story chatter in your head. I have good news for you! Most of what is said can be ignored or questioned, and there are ways to silence the mind. I'm not saying it's easy. I'm saying it can be done and that it's worth doing!

> *"There is nothing more important to true growth*
> *than realizing that you are not the voice of the mind*
> *- you are the one who hears it."*
> ~ Michael A. Singer, The Untethered Soul

QUIETING THE MIND
Non-stop internal chatter is a common complaint I hear from clients. "I can't sleep because of the constant talking in my head!" After questions to discern whether it is their own voice, or someone else's, we move on to learning how to quiet the mind. This takes practice and patience, and it comes with a warning: After the relief wears off, it feels really weird to have silence in your head!

1. The voice in your head is not you. You are the one hearing the voice.
2. The voice is part of the physical brain, the survival mechanism called the Critical factor (or ego?), and, in its efforts to keep you safe, it looks for things to fix. Since it always finds problems to fix, it is never content until you train it to be happy and quiet.

3. You, the one who hears the voice, can talk back to it and give it some love, "Oh, are you feeling afraid? Come here, and let me give you a hug." Pretend it's a small child and hold it tenderly. This is you (the soul), loving you (the critical factor in the physical mind), and the more you love every aspect of this physical self, the easier it is to live loved. Thereafter, the mind calms down and gets quiet.

4. Learn to question the thoughts through an inquiry process such as, "The Work" by Byron Katie. I cannot stress enough the importance of learning to question the validity of your (critical factor) thoughts.

5. The author of *The Untethered Soul*, Michael Singer, suggests that you imagine putting the voice outside of your body, giving it its own body and a funny name, and then spending the day listening to everything it has to say. It wouldn't be long before you wondered if this person was nuts and told them to go away. Yet, when you put that very same voice back inside your head, you believe everything it says. Enough! Learning to question your thoughts is an invaluable and important step to emotional wellness and living loved.

DISENGAGING THE VOICE IN YOUR HEAD:
I invite you to notice right now where your tongue is resting in your mouth. For most of us that will be on the roof of the mouth or behind the upper teeth. Next, I'm going to encourage you to take in a nice deep breath, pressing your tongue to the

roof of your mouth, and on the exhale, you intentionally let the tongue drop and rest into the lower jaw (that's where it is when you are asleep), and even let your lower jaw relax and go slack. Do this process several times, until you can notice the difference in your head. Even your shoulders will relax and feel as if they drop several inches. When the tongue is pressed to the roof of your mouth, the brain is in gear. This tongue position is like parking the car in a garage, leaving it in gear with a high idle, thus putting tension on the back wall. When you drop the tongue and relax the jaw, it has the effect of putting the brain in park. Everything will relax, even the voice I your head.

> *"The only permanent solution*
> *to your problems is to go inside*
> *and let go of the part of you*
> *that seems to have so many problems with reality."*
> ~ Michael A. Singer, *The Untethered Soul*

LISTEN TO SILENCE
There seems to be a general obsession for avoiding silence: music, television, smart phones, and texting. There is a constant external chatter that is used to chase away silence. Is there something you are afraid of? What might happen if you allowed more and more silence in your day?

When we have the courage to sit in silence, we might notice that there is a sacred stillness and a deep quiet behind everything.

This silence may be heard between every word, in the midst of bird song, and behind the breath. It is in this silence that we're able to hear the Beloved, and our own higher self, talking to us. Out of silence comes a knowing, an ability to hear things that really matter, and discovery of the deep longings of the heart. What might you hear if you allowed silence? Remember that you are loved and there is only love in the silence. Anything else is fear-based mind chatter to be hugged and then ignored.

I invite you to be in stillness and silence for one minute each day. Then, day by day, build up your courage until you are sitting or walking in silence for twenty minutes each day. Let Love Itself be your companion as you embrace silence.

Old worldview

- When I get uncomfortable with silence, I should fill it with noise.
- Silence is scary and should be avoided.

New worldview

- I am safe and loved.
- Silence is an invitation to listen.
- Silence is an invitation to love.

All the activity
the rush and struggle
so much noise
that crowds the ineffable

Allowing a moment's silence
on the edge of being still
a whisper of Love
beyond words.
~Marie Maguire

"Silence is the language of God,
all else is poor translation."
~ Rumi (Sufi)

"Silence is God's first language."
~ John of the Cross (Christian)

"Silence is a source of Great Strength."
~ Lao Tzu (Daoism)

"The best remedy for those who are
afraid, lonely or unhappy
is to go outside, somewhere where they can be quiet,
alone with the heavens, nature and God.
Because only then does one feel
that all is as it should be."
~ Anne Frank (a wise child)

BEFRIEND EMOTIONS

Emotions always follow thoughts around in the same way a dog's tail follows his body. The tail never gets out in front, no matter how the dog dances around! Thought comes first even if we aren't conscious of the content. If you want to change an emotion, change the thought or belief that inspired it. Or...

When the wave of an emotion flows over us, it is a natural impulse to grab onto it if it's pleasant, and push it away if it is uncomfortable. What I want you to know in your bones is that emotions are energy waves that want to flow through you. When you allow the energy to flow freely, you remain emotionally and physically healthy. When you resist, contract, or limit the emotion in any way, vital life energy is constricted, and you create dis-ease in your body and mind. When you restrict the flow long enough it creates a health crisis such as heart, liver, or intestinal challenges which warrant outside intervention.

Emotions are messengers that want you to pay attention to and heal something. Bypassing, ignoring, or rushing to spiritualize so you don't have to feel the pain, will prolong your journey to emotional wellness and create more suffering. Make emotions your friend because they have good intentions for you. They want to help you!

WHEN YOU FEEL ANY EMOTION ARISE, TAKE ACTION:

- Observe the emotion. Watch it without holding on to it, or adding to it with internal stories.
- Name it; don't claim it.

- "I am afraid" is a statement of being that influences negative body reaction.
- "I feel afraid" (anger, sadness...) allows for exploration without negative physical harm.
- Invite the emotion to express itself. Open your mouth and breathe, then keep on breathing intentionally throughout the full emotional expression. This process usually lasts only 90 seconds.
- On the exhale, give sound to the emotion: groan, growl, sigh, make raspberry noises, etc.
- Relax your shoulders and let them drop from around your ears.
- Hug and show compassion to yourself. Be your own loving best friend.
- Know that this emotion has everything to do with you and nothing to do with anyone else; no matter how convincing the story to which it is attached.
- Move your body through walking, gardening, running, dancing, or exercising, etc.
- After a while, use inquiry to question the story behind the emotion.
- Ask the emotion: What do you need to feel better? Do it, as long as harm comes to no one.
- Seek out professional support for guidance in working through to healing.

Example: Over several days, I felt a growing unease in my emotions. During a conversation with a friend (I'm an external processor), I discovered words to describe this feeling, "I feel lost and late, as if I'm expected somewhere, and have no idea how to get there." So, on my own, I sat and breathed into the emotion, allowed my shoulders to drop, and breathed into the thoughts that were inspiring my discomfort and suffering. I questioned whether it was even possible to *be* lost and late, within my current worldview. The answer was clear, and the feeling flowed on through. When I remember that I'm safe within Love Itself, I know that where I am is where I'm meant to be. Love always sees me through to the next step, safely, sanely, and with inspiration that knows how to move me at the right moment. Peace is the pal of Love Itself. They hang out together!

Example: An unfortunate misunderstanding occurred and the other person assumed I did this thing on purpose to offend. They called me vindictive and wouldn't listen for they already had their story firmly in place. Over the next few days I felt a series of emotions that I allowed to flow. I watched them cascade through until they got to anger. I felt the anger and asked it what it needed to feel better. It didn't want to expend the energy to explain, or try to fix the confusion. It only wanted to know what the threatened punishment was, so it could help me take empowered action. Done.

Using the above process can shorten many an emotional crisis, and also reveal to you when you need to seek outside assistance for support.

"Through an awareness of fear,
violence no longer becomes an option.
As fear is faced, sadness is encountered.

As sadness is encountered, loneliness is acknowledged.
As loneliness is acknowledged, emptiness is recognized.
As emptiness is recognized, a presence
of being is discovered.
As a presence of being is discovered
— consciousness awakens."
~ Matt Kahn

IS IT GUILT OR CONFUSION?

When we do something that seems like a stumble, something that we or society tells us is bad, wrong, or a mistake, I can't help wonder whether it would be more helpful to understand that the action came from a confused attempt to get love rather than from a flawed or sinful soul. Confusions don't warrant shame and punishment. They crack us open and inspire more opportunities to grow and learn. (Certainly, some acts of confusion may call for confinement, so that others are unharmed.)

I had a session with a life coach who was the second person to confirm that I "might have been an arrogant and judgmental spiritual teacher if I hadn't done such a good job of falling on my face again and again." My confusions have humbled me, taught me mercy and wisdom, and granted me a kinder and more loving spirit. I'm thankful for the confused actions and the lessons learned! In my personal experience, every one of my stumbles, big and small, has been a resource to bless, comfort, and help others along their way. A blessing indeed!

From a ground level perspective, here and now in this body, I highly recommend making amends wherever possible or paying it forward when it's not possible to make amends. From a higher perspective, how can one regret actions, however confused, that have transformed one's soul? Let yourself know, deep inside, that any seeming stumble is part of your particular dance to wholeness. I invite each of us to remove guilt and shame from our worldview and live freely within Love Itself. So, instead of feeling shame or guilt, or labeling yourself as bad, why not recognize your confused attempt to get love, shake yourself off, make amends when possible, and adjust your course to a wiser and more empowered action toward Love Itself?

All of my favorite people have been broken open by the heartache of confused actions. Something deep and precious takes place in the heart of those who make mistakes. In fact, so many spiritually good things happen from making mistakes, that I highly recommend that you go live out loud, make a few yourself, and let your heart get broken open in the process. I will gladly welcome you to the Happily Humbled Club!

Old worldview

- I'm a flawed and sinful soul, worthy of shame and punishment.
- When I do bad things it means I'm a bad person.

New worldview

- I'm a beautiful soul on a spiritual journey.
- Confusions on how to get the love we need are part of everyone's journey.
- My confusions humble me, expose my wounds, and teach me mercy and wisdom.
- I am in need of compassion, as is everyone else.

> *"Something very beautiful happens to people*
> *when their world has fallen apart;*
> *a humility, a nobility, a higher intelligence emerges*
> *at just the point when our knees hit the floor."*
> ~ Marianne Williamson

NAMING OURSELVES AND OTHERS

When someone asks us our name, or who we are, we often precede our self-declaration with "I am, I have, I always..." These are identity statements, words of creation and great power. Whatever we put after these words influences our minds and bodies down to the cellular level. When we use identity statements, we imply that the thing we're describing is part of us and as unchangeable as our DNA. Our words create our interior and exterior world.

When we name other people, **we freeze frame a moment in our experience of someone and call that image**

complete by assigning a name: stupid, lazy, rude, bully, and our society's current favorites, sociopath or narcissist. Too often, we focus on the negative description to define and identify who they are. "You are, they are, they always, they never..." These terms are related to the "I am" statement, and also carry great power, whether said aloud or not.

RESULTS OF NAMING OTHERS:

- You cease seeing a whole and complete person.
- It hyper-focuses your attention on the perceived negative trait.
- It energetically inspires more of the named quality (even if the named person doesn't know).
- You make them "other" than yourself and, therefore, less human.
- You blame them for your misery, rather than taking empowered action to meet your own needs.
- Your judgment creates constriction in your heart, to the point of closing it.
- From this constricted place, it is common to make poor decisions.
- It leads to some level of abandonment as empathy evaporates.
- Lacking empathy, you feel free to bully, abuse, or harm others (verbally or physically). You feel justified with no need for apology or amends.
- It often leads to shunning of friends, family, and whole groups of people.

- Your world gets smaller.
- It keeps you from seeing, "What else is possible?"

We are each so much more than any name or description could possibly reveal. Read that line over and over to let it sink in! You, I, and everyone else are much more than we can imagine.

So, what else is possible? How do you keep your heart and mind open? What process can you use to become conscious and stop naming others?

1. Decide you wish to become conscious and ask for divine assistance, "whatever it takes!"
2. When aware of naming someone, immediately turn that name back on yourself.
   - In that moment, you are being exactly what you are naming the other.
   - They are so mean / It's me that's being mean
   - They are selfish / It's me being selfish
   - They are fools / It's me being the fool
   - They're evil / It's me speaking evil
3. Ask yourself, "What do I expect the other person to give me?"
4. Then empower yourself and give to yourself what you need: love, kindness, appreciation, safety, mercy, compassion, empathy, etc.
5. Do your own internal work and healing, and if it's still necessary, have a nonviolent talk with the other person. Use no blame and ask for what you need.

Example: The name of "selfish" came into my mind when I was talking with a friend. I was able to turn it around and find my own selfishness. I discovered what it was that I needed, and then gave it to myself. A conversation about it was unnecessary, as the thing was resolved by empowering myself to meet my own need. Without this process, a brick of separation may have been put in a wall that could eventually destroy the relationship (shunning).

Example: Years ago, I had a friend with small children, one of whom I didn't like. As a result, I had assigned a negative name to the child in my mind. I never spoke the name aloud, yet my heart closed toward this child. Every time I was near, his mom informed me that he never acted that way around anyone else. I realized I was the adult here; accordingly I decided to open my heart and love this child. While the change in his behavior was dramatic, I'm the one who was truly transformed. **I fully understood that I had helped to create his negative behavior by the power of my naming him.** This experience opened my curiosity to how else I was influencing my world.

Example: Some years back, there was a group of people that didn't admire or respect me, and I felt their enmity. Whenever in their presence, no matter how hard I tried, I seemed to talk and behave in ways that supported their low view of me. In other situations, outside their presence, I would speak and act from a calm and sensible place. I realized that their low opinion of me was influencing my behavior. Because of this experience, I've learned how to energetically protect myself and limit this kind of external pressure. I'm grateful for the opportunity to learn so much from these souls, my teachers.

Example: As I've listened to people tell tales from their life, it is common to hear them name others as "narcissist" or "sociopath." I've seen the light dawn in their eyes as we discuss differing temperament traits, and how they display in work and relational situations. A so named sociopathic boss becomes a human being with opposite personality traits than the speaker. A feeler comes to understand a thinker. An intuitive realizes what it's like to live as a sensor. The artistic, upon discovering why the organizers get upset, learns how to maintain peace in their world. When we expand our knowledge base and open ourselves to different ways of being in the world, we discover empathy for our human interactions and we cease declaring negative names for ourselves and others.

Are there people who suffer from narcissism and sociopathy in the world? Yes, certainly, and I bet there are far fewer than those so named. It would be more effective, and helpful for world peace, to find those traits in our own shadow and embrace and heal that aspect within ourselves, so that we stop being triggered, or controlled by it, elsewhere.

Think about people in your life whom you've given negative labels. Explore the possibility that you're inspiring at least some of the negative behavior you say you can't stand. Explore how learning more about personalities could expand your compassion. How might you open your heart, and release the label--and thus the person--to more positive behavior? Elsewhere, we will explore how projecting labels onto other people reveals more about us than it does about them.

Old worldview

- People are only what we label them.
- My labels are correct and I should shun others.

New worldview

- People are so much more than what we see.
- My seeing of others is influenced by my own shadow.
- My labeling of others influences how they behave around me.
- Developing empathy will lead to more wisdom and peace in my world.
- There is so much to explore and understand about humanity.

> *"When you call people schizophrenic*
> *(lazy, stupid, narcissistic…),*
> *they are likely to live up to your label,*
> *You have stigmatized them.*
> *When you regard them as people who*
> *suffer episodes of schizophrenia,*
> *that they are more than their illness,*
> *then you give the healthy part a chance to grow."*
> ~ Ajahn Brahm

> *Don't be swift to label normal human traits as evil,*
> *for we're all frail, foolish and absurd in someone's eyes.*
> *The cure for such confusion is empathy.*
> ~ Marie Maguire

You Alone Choose Your Name

When another person names you (silly, dumb, know-it-all, narcissist, resistant ass, etc.), you have every right to refuse that name. You and you alone, have the right to choose your name and label your frailties. Feel free to name yourself, your traits, your strengths and weaknesses, as well as your personality, keeping in mind that the names you embrace increase the power of that thing you claimed for yourself. Be certain to claim only those things that help you grow toward love.

I know a person who claimed "Narcissist" for himself. Whether it was true or not, the claiming caused others to now see, experience, and respond to him as if he was that label.

What would happen, here and now, if you dropped all the old negative names? Both those that were given to you and those claimed by yourself: Thunk! See them, right there in front of you, in a pile, and then sweep them away. Receive a deep, cleansing breath and choose an empowered life of living loved.

> "… the moment I stand in reverence
> before every human being
> and see God in him —
> that moment I am free from bondage,
> everything that binds vanishes, and I am free."
> ~ Swami Vivekananda

KEEPING YOUR HEART OPEN

As you explore this concept and practice, it is helpful for you to become aware of the difference between an open and a closed heart. When you are happy, laughing, and hopeful then take notice of what your heart feels like in the center of your chest. When you are angry, sad, or resentful please notice what happens to your heart. Keep doing this process until you become aware of the decided difference of feeling in the mid-chest region.

It is possible, and even desirable, for health and wellness reasons, to keep your heart open no matter what emotion you experience.

AS SOON AS YOU FEEL THE BEGINNING OF CONSTRICTION IN YOUR MID-CHEST, DO THESE THINGS:

- Breathe and notice what feeling or experience is inspiring the constriction.
- Breathe the emotion or experience *into* the heart space.
- Invite, see, and feel the heart expanding to embrace the emotion/experience.
- Keep breathing in and expanding the heart.
- Your heart can expand as large as it needs to embrace this emotion/experience.
- From this expanded place, you have access to your heart and mind to make wise decisions.

Example: A strong emotion of loneliness came upon me. I sat, breathed in the loneliness, and watched my heart expand. My shoulders dropped, my breathing became deeper and more relaxed. I kept breathing in the loneliness until my heart contained it all. In this instance, higher wisdom came and showed me my connections to others and to all that is, and the loneliness dissolved. This process took only ten minutes, whereas, if I'd resisted and let my heart constrict, I could have been miserable for days or months.

Old worldview

- Feelings are scary things.
- There is such a thing as positive and negative feelings.
- I avoid feeling much of anything negative.
- I close my heart to keep myself safe.

New worldview

- Feelings are an energy that wants to flow.
- Feelings are messengers to help me heal something.
- I embrace the feeling and breathe through its full expression.
- I keep my heart open at all times. It is for my best and highest good.

> *"Emotional release is a potent way*
> *to regain a genuine experience of the moment.*
> *Tears are God's heart-shield wipers.*
> *They clear the dirt from our heart so*
> *we can see the path clearly.*
> *Let our quest for spiritual expansion*
> *begin with emotional authenticity.*

Nothing to hide, nowhere to hide it."
~ Jeff Brown

I APOLOGIZE

As stated previously, any word we use after the powerful "I am" statement becomes the declaration of our being. For example, saying the common phrase "I'm sorry" declares that I am a sorry human being, which immediately affects our physical and emotional body. Sorry becomes our statement of being, and this affects our physiology down to the cellular level. Let's not do that.

IT IS MORE HELPFUL, EFFECTIVE, AND TRUE TO SAY:

- I apologize, please forgive me.
- My heart goes out to you.
- So sorry (said all by itself).
- My heart is with you in this loss.
- I feel for you and your family.
- I hold you in my prayers.
- What may I do to support you?
- How may I best help you?
- What do you need most at this time?
- Or give a long, quiet hug and use your eyes to say it all.

No Problem

"No problem," seems to be the current most common response when someone says, "Thank you." Saying "no problem" *is* a problem because, according to hypnotherapy research and client experience, our subconscious mind doesn't register the no. The message that gets through to our subconscious mind is the following: we were a problem, could have been a problem, or may be a problem in the future.

Another example of *no* in action is: "Don't drink that red Kool Aid over the white carpet!" In effect, you just told them to drink the Kool Aid over the white carpet, and you get mad at them for doing so. Rewording is powerful: "Please drink the Kool Aid in the kitchen." The mind gets the message and there is less chance of a mess.

So, instead of saying "no problem", what if we bring into play some of these happy and positive responses?

What will life be like when we respond with…?

- You're welcome
- My pleasure
- Any time
- It was fun
- Let's do it again
- A smile and nod

Recently I was shopping at a grocery store and asked an employee for help. After getting the assistance, I thanked him and he said, "You are most welcome!" I stopped in my tracks and thanked him again for such a positive and warm response. The person proceeded to tell me how much he disliked the common "no problem" answer most people give.

Over the next week keep your ears tuned to all the times you hear, or are tempted to say, "No problem." Play with a new response until you find the one that feels good to you and watch how others react to your positive words. This is you using simple words to create a more positive world!

Old worldview

- How I say things doesn't matter.
- If a majority of people use a phrase, it must be okay.

New worldview

- My words create my world.
- My words inspire a positive response in others.
- There is great magic in how I say things.

FORGIVENESS

The transcendent work of forgiveness is like the peeling of an onion, and it's often done one layer at a time. Recently, I was doing inner work on forgiving someone who had passed away years ago. This deeper layer was tougher than others, and I kept going back to judgment, "How could you be so blind?" Eventually, I felt inspired to adjust my viewpoint to a higher perspective and take the perceived offenses down to their most basic level, which is unconsciousness. The offending words and actions came from a place of unconsciousness. (Indeed, that could be said about every confused word or action.)

As I embraced the idea of unconsciousness, in an instant everything changed. I was easily able to find that place in myself where I have been, and done, and said things from unconsciousness. The need to forgive dissolved into the light of acceptance and love. **"I am you, you are me, and we have all been unconscious."** Both of us were set free in that moment and my heart was mended. Blessed be the journey to Love!

To forgive others, we need to break down the offense into its most basic form, and find that same common confusion within ourselves. And believe me, it is there. Then, we need to digest the fact that they didn't do that (unconscious) thing because they were evil, no-good monsters. They did that (unconscious) thing because they are on the same journey to consciousness as we ourselves and are trying to find their way. **We don't do unconscious things because we are evil. We do them because we are confused about how to get the love we need.**

"I am you, you are me, and we have all been unconscious. I forgive your confused actions, as I forgive myself the same."

Blessed be the journey to Love!

Old worldview

- People don't deserve forgiveness.
- I would never be as bad/stupid/evil as they are.

New worldview

- An unforgiving attitude closes my heart. Forgiveness opens my heart.
- All wrongdoing comes from a place of confusion and unconsciousness.
- We have all been confused and unconscious.
- All of us need forgiveness at one time or another.
- Whether they ask for it or not, I need to forgive them, so I can be set free.
- Even when I forgive I can keep myself safe from dangerous actions.

> *"He who is devoid of the power to forgive*
> *is devoid of the power to love.*
> *There is some good in the worst of us,*
> *and some evil in the best of us.*
> *When we discover this, we are less*
> *prone to hate our enemies."*
> ~ Martin Luther King, Jr.

What to Do When Offended

When someone says or does something that offends you in any way, there are things you need to do before spouting off words of anger and hurt, or going to the extreme of shunning.

Your response to any event is all about you. (I keep repeating this idea in different ways because I want it to sink into your bones!) No matter what someone else said or did, your reaction is all about what is going on, and what needs to be healed, inside of you. If you didn't believe the thought brought up by this incident, you simply wouldn't be offended.

For instance:

1. If I made fun of you for having bright green hair and you don't have bright green hair, you would laugh, wonder about my sanity, give me a funny look, and move on.
2. If you do have bright green hair, and love the attention, this comment won't offend.
3. If my making fun of your green hair brings up something you have hidden in your shadow (crazy, weird, stupid, not enough), you will react with strong emotion and may want to retaliate with harsh words or shunning.

So, I say it again, *your reaction is all about you.* Deal with yourself first. Embrace your shadow self. Love, heal, and forgive your own inner confusions. Only then, if needed and called for, will you be able to communicate in a way that brings new life to the relationship. **"Wow, when you said/did (....) it brought up old stuff for me, and it gave me the opportunity to heal myself. Thank you! And, from now on, I'd prefer ...."**

I invite you to explore your suffering by using some form of inquiry. The works of Eckhart Tolle, Adyashanti, Gangaji, and Byron Katie are great resources. Or you may choose to see a coach or counselor who is trained to help you explore the belief that is causing you to suffer. You may also do the shadow or mirror work mentioned elsewhere in this book.

"Everything that irritates us about others
can lead us to an understanding of ourselves."
~ Carl Jung

When I love and forgive myself first,
it becomes easier to do the same for others.
~ Marie Maguire

WRONG WAY AROUND

It seems, in the old collective worldview, when people face ruin, devastation, difficulties, and disturbing emotional challenges, they are thought to be less than, other than, or in need of drugs, therapy, or being hidden away in institutions. I have found on my own journey, and in my work with many others, that these events are truly spiritual emergencies, and therefore, a call to transformation. They are revolutionary moments, an opportunity to open, and so they are a precious gift!

Comfortable? Easy? NO!

Good, wondrous, evolutionary, scary? YES!

Instead of chastising, drugging, or hiding these people, we ought to honor them, surround them with tender loving care and support, and invite open spiritual explorations (worldview expansion). Point them away from fear and towards Love Itself. At the very least, we could explain to them that what they are experiencing is honorable and often leads to good things when one follows love and abstains from fear.

Old worldview

- Having emotional problems means there is something deeply wrong with me.
- Fear and shame belong to people who have mental problems.

New worldview

- A spiritual emergency is a loving call for transformation.
- Here is an opportunity to open and grow. It is truly an honor and a gift!

"Ruin and pain are a gift;
they are the road to transformation."
~ Elizabeth Gilbert

EVERYTHING (AND EVERYONE) IS OUR TEACHER

Instead of pointing our fingers and labeling challenging people as enemy, bully, narcissist, ass, troublemaker, and so on, what if we had a whole new viewpoint? What if everything (and everyone) that trips us up or pushes our buttons creates an opportunity for us to look inside and heal a part of our self? As we allow this worldview to be true for us, then everyone becomes our teacher. Imagine, for even a moment, that this idea is true, and imagine that the worst of your experiences occurred to teach you something that, at a deeper spiritual level, you wanted to learn. What if each character in this life experience agreed to help you learn this lesson, and each did it out of love for you?

Imagine a conversation that may have taken place in spirit form, before this life. It could go something like this: "Hey friend, I'm going back into body to learn more about forgiveness. I may even use what I learn to help others along the way. Friend, do you want to help me with this project?" "Sure," says your friend, "I could play the role of your childhood buddy that betrays you and becomes spiteful." "Thank you!" you say, and you go through the veil of forgetting as you enter your mother's womb. Then, this spiritual friend presents you with the previously agreed opportunity to learn how to forgive.

What if it happens this way? How might this change your thoughts? Your judgments? Your ability to forgive? Whether it's true or not, how much better might your life be by embracing this idea?

Old worldview

- Enemies and troublemakers are to be avoided.
- They are bad and they bring bad things into my life.

New worldview

- Everyone is my teacher.
- I may have asked them to help me learn something new.
- I am not, and never will I be, a victim.
- Challenging people and events invite me to look inside and heal aspects of myself.
- All difficulties are an invitation and a gift.

> *"View your life with Kindsight*
> *Instead of slapping your forehead and asking:*
> *"What was I thinking?"*
> *Breathe and ask yourself the kinder question:*
> ***"What was I learning?"***
> ~ Karen Salmansohn

MEANING MAKING MACHINES

I've discovered in my personal and client work, over and over again, that it's not what happens to us that matters. It is the meaning (the internal story) that we apply to the event that makes all the difference. The meaning that we create builds our worldview, through which we then experience the world, and it becomes the vessel that holds our suffering.

For example, I've had clients with many challenging life experiences who have let those times flow through them without giving them meaning. "It is what it is." Other clients, who have had fewer or less momentous challenges, have made a mountain of meaningful decisions that have caused deep suffering. Why might that be? I believe these decisions are influenced by the chosen challenges and path for this particular life. Personally, I'm in the group that gave a lot of meaning to the challenging life events, and it's taken me on an interesting healing journey.

A sure way to live loved is to be actively aware of this process and let events flow through you without having to label them with meaning. Be present in the moment with what is, accept it as it is, and deal with it in an empowered way, without making any judgments.

HOW TO MAKE MEANING THAT CAUSES SUFFERING:

1. An event happens containing an indisputable fact (car crash).
2. You decide that the event means _____.

a. (I am, the world is, women are, men are, people are, always, never, this is bad...)

b. And you suffer.

3. From then on, anything that consciously or unconsciously reminds you of that event has you respond from the decision that was made, as if the meaning you gave it is the only one possible. And you suffer.

   a. Many of these meanings were decided before the age of 6-10 years old, when you had fewer emotional, spiritual, or intellectual resources. Even as an adult you add meaning to events.

   b. These meanings inhabit your worldviewand are the screen through which you see and experience everything and everyone.

   c. Every moment of suffering that you experience can be traced back to one of these meanings within your worldview.

How to let events flow through you:

1. An event happens that contains an indisputable fact (car crash).

2. You breathe deeply, drop your shoulders, and are present with what is happening in that moment.

3. Accept what is, as it is, and do what needs to be done to handle the event.

4. Allow no labels or judgments to form. "This challenge is part of life."

5. Employ sayings that keep you in a place of peace.
   a. All things work together for my good.
   b. I'm loved and safe within Love Itself.
   c. Whether I live or die, I'm safe.
   d. All is for fun and for learning.
   e. I know nothing for sure.
   f. If negative judgment arises, ask: What else is possible?

> *When I feel afraid, it shows I'm not fully convinced*
> *that Love Itself is really good. I'm not*
> *trusting God's love for me.*
> ~ Marie Maguire

> *"When the chaos becomes safety to you,*
> *then you know you're seeing God clearly."*
> ~ Caroline Myss

THIS IS GOOD/THAT IS BAD!

May it be our goal to stop labeling everything as either good or bad. On one hand, we have no way to know for sure whether it really is good or bad. On the other hand, we do ourselves and others a disservice by limiting everything to black-and-white thinking. This journey to a new and expanded worldview will eventually get us to the idea that **we don't know anything for sure**. It feels strange at first, yet it's a very good place to be!

A favorite Zen story that illustrates this concept:

Maybe

Once upon a time, there was an old farmer who had worked his crops for many years. One day his horse ran away. Upon hearing the news, his neighbors came to visit. "Such bad luck," they said sympathetically.

"Maybe," the farmer replied.

The next morning the horse returned, bringing with it three other wild horses. "How wonderful," the neighbors exclaimed.

"Maybe," replied the old man.

The following day, his son tried to ride one of the untamed horses, was thrown, and broke his leg. The neighbors again came to offer their sympathy on his misfortune.

"Maybe," answered the farmer.

The day after, military officials came to the village to draft young men into the army. Seeing that the son's leg was broken, they passed him by. The neighbors congratulated the farmer on how well things had turned out.

"Maybe," said the farmer.

The safest, most loving, and most peaceful place to be in your worldview is to realize that you know nothing at all, about anything. Let go of judgments and you go a long way into peace of mind. Trust that you are loved by Love Itself and leave it at that.

Old worldview

- I know when an event is good or bad.
- I can be certain that my label (good or bad) is right.

New worldview

- I know nothing for sure.
- Everything that comes my way comes through love first.
- All things work together to help me on my journey to living loved.

> *"When nothing is sure, everything is possible."*
> ~ Margaret Drabble

"YES, BUT"

You may become aware of receiving potentially great ideas and suggestions for healing or fixing what ails you, whether from your relative, counselor, pastor, or best friend. Even so, you may find yourself saying, "Yes, but...." followed by a string of excuses that detail why you can't or won't do this thing. Whenever you use the "yes, but..." you are arguing for your limitations. **When you argue for your limitation, you get to keep it!**

Here's the surprise! I invite you to keep your limitations, and to stay right where you are for as long as you need to be there. Get all that you came for out of this particular challenge and move on only when you are ready. What will it be like to be honest with yourself and others, and to stop wasting energy on complaints that inspire advice-giving, and on excuses that create frustration all around?

"Nothing ever goes away until it has taught us
what we need to know."
~ Pema Chodron

⌒

ADVICE GIVING

If you are the one who is offering the advice for fixing or heal-ing, may I say that it's vital that you refrain (stop it!). If you are willing, listen without judgment, ask questions, be curious about their journey, and if appropriate and loving, help them discover the benefits of the current challenge. People will be free only as, and when, they are ready to be free. Therefore, when you find yourself getting frustrated, know that you have decided when and how their freedom should happen. Get back into your own business and hold a space of love for them.

Advice giving is a rather violent sport, where the receiver is always on the losing end. The advice giver takes a superior position of power and declares what the other should, could, or ought to do to fix his/her troubles. According to Parker Palmer advice giving is "a strategy for abandoning each other while ap-pearing to be concerned." What is more, the receiver often goes away feeling unheard (unloved), and nowhere closer to finding their way through.

What else is possible? The best service you can render is to hold a space of love and to trust Love Itself to guide people on their journey. I invite you to know that all is well, and all will be well at the proper time. Encourage him/her to freely express their struggles, so that they may eventually hear their own inner wise teacher, who knows what is best.

What happens? When people realize that they are received with love, and are thus safe to express all the confused emotions and thoughts that go with their struggle, then they may dig deeper into the roots and find the buried truths. And you get to be a witness.

We are each on a sacred journey. Each challenge we face is a perfect setup, an opportunity, to discover the freedom of love. Do you have the courage and gentleness to allow others to walk safely? Can you, will you, provide a safe circle of trust? If, for any reason, you're unable to offer this safety, be upfront and let the person know. Either way, you are keeping them safe from spiritual violence.

"In a circle of trust,
where confronting and correcting are forbidden,
we feel safe enough for the inner
teacher [Love Itself]
to confront and correct us."
~ Parker Palmer

*"Do the best you can until you know better.
Then when you know better, do better."*
~ Maya Angelou

WAKING UP

Until we know better, until we make the choice to stop living in the past or future, we are living asleep. We grow up asleep, marry asleep, work asleep, and die asleep. We're trance walking through life and missing out on the whole, glorious, and delightful reasons for living. Those reasons are found throughout this book.

There is some discussion as to whether we need pain and suffering to wake us up out of our trance, or whether we can get there in a more peaceful fashion. My personal and professional experience says that pain and suffering are usually involved. In fact, I believe that waking up may be the entire purpose of pain and suffering. Let's embrace our opportunities!

Spirituality means waking up. The healing of emotional wounds means waking up. Wholeness means being aware, being in touch with one's heart, mind, body and soul, and knowing that no matter the outer circumstances, that "all is well" because of Love Itself.

However, I invite you to wake up at your own pace. No one likes to be rushed out of sleep and into alertness. When you are ready to make your commitment to wake up and live in this moment, you will invite Love Itself to guide you to the places you need to go, the books you need to read, and to the people who will assist and teach you. Let love be your guide-post, for love is the only real thing, and only love will satisfy your longings.

Old worldview

- Everyone should be at the same place of development and understanding.
- Everyone should be where I am on the journey.
- People need to be pushed along or judged as wrong.

New worldview

- We each wake up or move forward at just the right moment.
- It's an honor to hold a space of love for another.
- My spiritual way and timing are best for me and no one else.

> *"(Man)... is so anxious about the future*
> *that he does not enjoy the present;*
> *the result being that he does not live*
> *in the present or the future;*
> *he lives as if he is never going to die,*
> *and then dies having never really lived."*
> ~ Dalai Lama

> *"We can ignore even pleasure.*
> *But pain insists upon being attended to.*
> *God whispers to us in our pleasures,*
> *speaks in our conscience,*

but shouts in our pains: it is his
megaphone to rouse a deaf world."
~ C. S. Lewis

"I walked a mile with Pleasure;
She chattered all the way,
But left me none the wiser
For all she had to say.
I walked a mile with Sorrow
And ne're a word said she;
But oh, the things I learned from her
When sorrow walked with me."
~ Robert Browning Hamilton

"Waking up is unpleasant, you know.
You are nice and comfortable in bed.
It's irritating to be woken up.
That's the reason the wise guru
will not attempt to wake people up."
~ Anthony de Mello

RELATIONSHIPS

As with everything else that occurs in our life, relationships are about fun and learning. What if our partners, parents, friends, and enemies are people we asked to share this life with us, so we may learn from one another? They're our teachers.

THE GIFTS OF RELATIONSHIP:

- They mirror our attitudes back to us, giving us the opportunity to grow.
- They poke our shadows which make us want to judge the other person instead of looking inside to face our own issues
- They won't/can't/don't give us things that we ought to be giving ourselves.
- They push us to learn, grow, and expand. The presented opportunity can be very uncomfortable.
- If we allow it, they give us chances to learn about forgiveness, grace, mercy, kindness, and unconditional love.

Everything we do, think, and are in our relationships comes from either love or fear. All actions and thoughts inspired by fear come from a place of confusion and result in suffering. Our confused actions are an attempt to get love. Our confusion produces more confusion, until we have suffered enough to declare a halt and commit to do whatever it takes to be in relationship with the real source of love. Thus we to learn to live loved, turn into love ourselves, and discover how to truly be available in relationships.

Find gratitude for all relationships that come your way, for they are a gift.

If we shun our teachers, how will we ever learn?
New teachers come again and again,

until we embrace the learning.
~ Marie Maguire

GET ME OUT OF HERE!

When pressures build and troubles mount, we often long for escape and pray prayers of desperation, the essence of which is "Get me out of this (job, relationship, financial trouble)!"

At this point, I'm inviting you to expand your worldview to consider that this pressure or trouble is here to bring you a gift. A gift, I say. Instead of trying to get out of it, what would your life be like if you invited "this challenge" to stay **for as long as it takes** to teach you what you need to know?

How will this new prayer shift your energy and attitudes? How will it open your heart to all the riches within the challenge? What if, instead of fear and rejection, it is the energy of love and peace that moves you forward?

Prayer: Don't let this (job, relationship, friendship...) end until I gain all that is to be learned.

Example: As with everything in this book, I learned this gem several times from personal experience. One time, I was working as a social worker for a community service agency. I ran seven programs, and the stress was beyond what I felt I could handle. During one of those "get me out of here" prayers, it seemed that

God came and asked me if I had learned everything I was supposed to learn from this situation. With a big exhale, and lots of requests for strength, I prayed, "God, don't let this job end until I've gained all I came here to learn." I was amazed at the immediate drop in stress, and there was even a surge of excitement that God had good things in mind. Eventually, I left that job for an even better one, yet only when both God and I were good and ready. I left when it was time, rather than an attempt to escape.

Example: In financial challenge, I learned to pray, "Don't let this challenge end until it has taught me all you (we) intend."

Example: In challenging relationship: "Don't let me run away. Help me learn all I came for."

Caution: Of course, this idea doesn't include situations where you're in danger. Find the courage and help you need to move away from danger, and then from a safe place do any inner work that needs doing.

Old worldview

- It is best to leave challenging relationships.
- If it's difficult then it isn't good, right or healthy.

New worldview

- All real relationships have challenging times.
- If it isn't challenging then one or both of us aren't being real.

- Difficulties are an opportunity to grow as individuals and as a team.
- I choose to stay until I have a clear, nonjudgmental release to go.

"If you are irritated by every rub,
how will your mirror be polished?"
and

"When someone beats a rug,
the blows are not against the rug,
but against the dust in it."
~ Rumi

STAY OR LEAVE RELATIONSHIPS?

Each relationship situation (lovers, parent/child, friends, or family) has a gift and a positive intention for us. Instead of trying to get away or escape the difficulties, let us pray that this situation will not end until we've gained all there is to gain. That doesn't mean that we will never leave or allow distance. It means that it shifts our focus from escape to trusting that this relationship may be for our best in this moment.

Within relationship there is so much to be learned that can wake us up. There are many opportunities for poking all the parts of us that need to grow, heal, and come alive: personality, temperament styles, love languages, strengths/weaknesses, internal/external processing, communication challenges and nonviolence, introversion/extroversion, different states of neurological tuning (sensitivity), power, empowerment, differing worldviews, states of awakening, and more. What better system could there be for helping us with this awakening than relationship?

Fear: When we leave a relationship out of fear, or out of a desire for escape, Love Itself may find another way to teach us the lesson(s) provided by the first opportunity. In this way, we go round and round the same relationship challenges until we heal our long time wounds, and discover what we need to learn.

Love: When we stay until we have learned all there is to learn, and we feel released to move forward out of love, compassion, and forgiveness, then we are truly free to move on and embrace a higher way of being.

One thing I know for sure is that we can't get from anyone else what we don't give first to ourselves. If we want love, peace, warmth, and affection in a relationship, we must first give it to ourselves, in order to then give it to them. What they give back is their business, and we get to choose (from a place of love) whether to stay and participate or not.

Also, for a relationship to survive and thrive, it takes two people who are willing to do the work, to live consciously, and to embrace the higher ways of being. If only one person is willing, then not much can be done. Still, let all "farewells" be gracious and peaceful, for one day a miracle may happen (in one or both), and they may walk through the door once more.

"Your task is not to seek for love,
but merely to seek and find all the
barriers within yourself
that you have built against it."
~ Rumi

"A relationship is not about holding hands
while you understand each other,
It's about having lots of misunderstandings
and still not leaving each other's hands."
~ Unknown

SHUNNING OUR TEACHERS

Shunning (sometimes called "ghosting"): To keep away from a place, person, object, etc., from motives of dislike or caution, etc.; to avoid.

Shunning of family and friends is far too common nowadays and probably deserves many books on the topic. I won't be writing any of those books. Nonetheless, I do want to touch on the subject. I must confess that I've done my share of shunning and I've been shunned as well. I can say, from both sides, that neither is inspired by love, nor generates love. If, as we've been exploring, difficulties are challenges with the purpose of helping us grow, then how does shunning the persons who present the growth opportunity help us in any way? It is fear that produces shunning. It is a misunderstanding of the purpose of difficulties. It is a running away from opportunities to grow. It can even be spiritual arrogance.

Of course, shunning creates its own opportunities to grow. And other teachers may be sent our way, again and again, until we open our hearts and grow. However, why not stick with the first opportunity, call out for help from Love Itself, and let love be your guide to wholeness?

SHORT TERM BENEFITS OF SHUNNING PEOPLE:

- Relief of pressure
- Self-righteousness (they're bad, I'm good)
- Feeling powerful or superior (I showed them!)
- Temporary feeling of safety

WHAT IS REALLY HAPPENING WHEN YOU SHUN PEOPLE?

- Your heart squeezes closed
- You've "other-ized" another human being
- Loss of compassion and empathy for another

- Loss of relationship and connection
- Your world gets smaller
- A feeling of exhaustion develops
- May result in physical dis-ease
- You draw in other teachers
- Lessons may get more difficult
- Shunning may lead to being shunned

Come, let us love one another with a love that hopes for the best, seeks out new strategies, opens our hearts, broadens our understanding, and discovers safe ways to stay connected.

STRATEGIES TO STAY CONNECTED:

1. Pray: "I request a most benevolent outcome in my relationship with _____."
2. "May I be the love, kindness, and affection I seek."
3. "Open my heart and mind that I may cooperate with Spirit. Don't let this situation end until I've gained all I've come here to learn."
4. Recognize that the judgment you place on the other is also living within yourself, so do the shadow work presented elsewhere in this book.
5. Your stories about this person, and the events involved, say more about you than about them. So do inquiry and learn to question your stories until you get to a fact on which you may then take action.
6. The communication style that has led to this desire to shun a loved one is often laced with verbal violence and a lack

of clarity surrounding your needs, so embrace nonviolent communication to become proficient at loving yourself and the other with your words.

7. Use your nonviolent voice to ask aloud for what you need.
8. Avoid naming the other (narcissist...) and keep your heart open.
9. Send waves of love from your heart to theirs, every day. "Blessed be _____" (each person involved).

After giving all of this sincere and determined effort, if the other person doesn't cooperate, then you may wish to allow some distance, while yet keeping your heart and mind open for "What else is possible?" Hold open hope for a spiritual revolution, within either or both, which may one day make relationship possible once again.

> *"However mean your life is, meet it and live it;*
> *do not shun it and call it hard names.*
> ~ Henry David Thoreau

> *"Not by blaming the world, not by shunning the world,*
> *but only by loving the world can I have peace of mind."*
> ~ Sri Chinmoy

> *If we must shun something, let it be ignorance,*
> *hatred, and fear within ourselves.*
> ~ Marie Maguire

BREAKING OPEN

The negative intent of any suffering we experience is for us to close down our hearts and collapse into fear and resentment. This process is what I refer to as "breaking closed." The positive intent of suffering is for our worldview to be broken open and expanded to include a higher understanding and awareness. The choice to be broken open or broken closed is ours alone. Our willingness to do the following depends on which way it goes.

1. **Progressive opening of our heart through gratitude**
   a. Let your awareness settle into your heart and invite it to open and expand.
   b. Breathe full body breaths and allow your heart to feel what comes next.
   c. I invite you to fully imagine, feel, and express gratitude for sweet innocent things like babies, kittens, and puppies.
   d. Extend this gratitude to include sunlight, warm showers, and chocolate.
   e. Expand gratitude to embrace loved ones, family, friends, and community.
   f. Now open your heart fully and express gratitude for the things that have challenged and frustrated you: accidents, denials, loss, and betrayal. (Yep, I'm serious about this one.)
   g. Let your heart expand to fully embrace all these things. Breathe them into your heart and, if you allow

it, the heart will always be larger than any challenge that comes your way.

Gratitude helps expand our awareness to include the possibility that we are loved and that all is well, no matter how things look or feel on the surface. Gratitude also shows that we trust God/Universe to provide what we need and turn all things around for our good. When we keep our hearts open, with gratitude, the world becomes a better place. Our brains switch our awareness away from separation and remind us that we are all interconnected.

Breaking open or breaking closed is a choice we each get to make. Trusting in love, that all is well even in our pain, makes all the difference.

Old worldview

- Closing my heart is the best response to suffering.
- Closing down is a natural response to difficulties.

New worldview

- Opening my heart is the best response to everything.
- I'm deeply aware of my heart's response to life.
- I choose to keep my heart open and soft.
- Gratitude reminds me that all is well in my world.
- Believing I'm loved shows itself through gratitude for all things.

"The same sun which melts butter also hardens clay."
~ Origen of Alexandria

I LEAVE YOU FREE TO BE YOURSELF

Anyone living as a human being knows what it's like to be loved conditionally. Even if the words aren't spoken, we know what it feels like to have the energy of conditions placed on our acceptance.

I LOVE YOU:

- if you get good grades,
- if you don't bother me with your feelings,
- if you make my life peaceful and fun,
- etcetera to infinity!

This conditional love gives us lots of opportunities to learn confusions. Before we find the way out we usually get small glimpses of unconditional love from friends, family, coaches, or any other person who knows the way. Once you learn and embrace unconditional love for yourself, then you can be that love for others who so desperately need it. We all need it!

It takes loving yourself to feel safe enough to allow someone to be themselves. God has this kind of unconditional love for us. Can we, will we, be open to giving this kind of love to ourselves and others?

WHAT DOES UNCONDITIONAL LOVE LOOK LIKE?

- I embrace and celebrate who you are – no need to hide.
- I have empathy for your confusions.
- I'm curious about what makes you tick!
- You are free to have a different worldview.
- I use nonviolent communication to communicate everything.
- I love you without an agenda.

Love yourself unconditionally and you will be free to love your neighbor and God.

"I leave you free to be yourself,
to think your thoughts,
to indulge your taste, follow your inclinations,
behave in any way that you decide is to your liking."
~ Anthony De Mello

"All I want from you is to trust me
with what little you can,
and grow in loving people around you
with the same love I share with you.
It's not your job to change them, or to convince them.
You are free to love without an agenda."
~ Wm. Paul Young

SELF-WORTH

Our ideas of self-worth are often derived from what we have, what we can do, what we look like, and/or how influential we are. A partial list of self-worth ideas could include looks, smarts, body shape, education, job, family ties, house, car, spouse, and so on. When we take an honest look at those things, we notice that every single one can be taken away from us by others or by circumstances. They will all be taken from us by time itself.

When we place the platform of our self-worth on any of the things that may be taken away, our self-worth is on unsteady ground, and we must be on the defensive to look out for ma-rauders. This shaky emotional ground often leads to insecu-rity, defensiveness, emotional instability, and anxiety, to name a few.

Example: If I base my self-worth on my intelligence, then I will tend to be unconsciously defensive when anyone comes along who is more intelligent than I, and I will try to knock the other person down a peg. Or if my intelligence is dimin-ished because of illness or accident, my self-value is shattered. It doesn't have to be this way.

What else is possible? I have found that the only thing that cannot and will not ever be shaken or removed is God's uncon-ditional delight and love. It is yours. You don't have to earn it. It cannot be lost. No one has more of that love than you. Even when you get confused, are injured, face illness, or mess up, it's still yours. It is solid ground. *It is the only solid ground.*

If you have trouble accessing or experiencing that kind of love, I invite you to play with a pile of puppies or a cadre of kittens. Hold a newborn in your arms to feel the joyous and gentle tenderness that arises and has nothing to do with being earned. Allow this kind of unconditional love to soak deeply into your heart, and know that God's love is magnified by a million and directed at you. Allow Love Itself embrace you, to fill all the corners of your being. Let love become who you are.

Unsteady ground or a sure and unshakable foundation—the choice is yours.

Old worldview

* My value is based on what I have: good looks, money, intelligence, etc.
* I need to be defensive so as not to lose my self-worth.
* I have a right to fiercely defend things on which I place my value.

New worldview

* My value is based on who I am within Love Itself.
* My value can never be shaken or taken from me.
* I am at peace within this unconditional love.

- I am loved and I am love itself.
- I'm on steady, immovable ground.

"You can only lose something that you have,
but you cannot lose something that you are..."
~ Eckhart Tolle

"A conviction that you are a (child) of God
gives you a feeling of comfort in your self-worth.
It means that you can find strength in
the balm of Christ [Love Itself].
It will help you meet the heartaches and challenges
with faith and serenity."
~ James E. Faust

Truth Speaking

"I have to speak my truth." There is some truth in that statement, and there is also much opportunity for emotional and verbal violence. First, what exactly do we mean here by "truth"?

Here are three very different options:

- Facts that are basic and unadorned
- Stories (our interpretation of basic facts) that are inspired by our worldview
- Emotions that boil over into harsh words

I agree that it's important to know and speak what is true (facts). It is also important to recognize and honor the emotions that spring up from our internal stories. Any kind of truth, when bottled up, causes vital energy to be constricted and dis-ease to form in our minds and bodies. It eventually bubbles over into unhealthy, confused words and actions.

The trouble with our truth (emotions and stories) is that it is mostly based on our limited worldview rather than fact. Remember, facts are indisputable and stories are anything we add on top of a fact. If you had a different worldview, your truth would also be different. Therefore, your truth is not everyone's truth and it can be full of hurtful words that don't need to be said aloud.

If something is bothering you to the point that you feel the pressure to speak your truth, the person who most needs to hear it is you. **Tell yourself your truth.** Work out your inner struggles. Embrace your emotions and discover your internal stories. Get help from a friend or coach. Have loving souls walk with you. Heal what needs to be healed. And, even then, the things that are best communicated aloud are the facts and the empowered action inspired by knowing your truth.

"After doing a lot of thinking, I realize that this (relationship, job, friendship, school, etc.) isn't what I need at this time. I apologize for any inconvenience and upset this causes, and I wish you the very best. Please forgive me, and let me move on gracefully."

IF YOU MUST GIVE A REASON, KEEP TO THE FACT SIDE OF TRUTH:

1. You want children, and I don't. We aren't a good fit.
2. This job requires extroverted energy, and I'm deeply introverted.
3. This friendship requires more than I have to give right now.
4. The school doesn't have the support programs I need at this time.
5. I was sexually abused as a child.

HERE ARE REASONS LACED WITH EMOTIONAL OR STORIED TRUTH:

1. I think you (or I) would be a terrible parent, and I never loved you anyways.
2. You ask for a stupid amount of client contact and schmoozing.
3. I can't stand how you drain every last bit of energy from me.
4. The arrogance of the teachers in my area of study is intolerable.
5. My family is evil and all of my suffering is their fault.

Be a truth teller, yes! However, **let it be the facts and the required action that you say aloud**. When you stick to the facts and actions, you can build a new and empowered life on those. When you share your raw truth laced with verbal violence, you create even more violence in your life and in the world.

"Today I bent the truth to be kind,
and I have no regrets,
for I am far more sure of what is kind
than I am of what is true."
~ Robert Brault

EMBRACING THE SHADOW

All of our lives, from infancy on, we get feedback from others on what is acceptable and what isn't. You know what I mean. We get a look, a verbal smack, a non-verbal sigh, or even an uncomfortable feeling, and we know in our bones that whatever we said or did was undesirable. Scary! Our very lives are dependent on these people, so we pay close attention and get rid of whatever isn't approved. What we do with all of those objectionable feelings and traits is stuff them into a bag that hangs at our back. This bag is our shadow.

Until we know better, we think that everything back there in our shadow should stay in the dark and be kept hidden forever. If we let those things be seen, we dread rejection and fear, and it may even cause the end of our world. The trouble is that we spend an enormous amount of energy keeping our shadow hidden. We move and maneuver, lie, and do whatever it takes to keep those "undesirable or shameful" traits out of sight. It's exhausting and pointless because, actually, we are often the only ones who aren't aware of what is hidden in that bag.

That's right! Other people can usually see what we are unconsciously trying to hide. In fact, we are telling them all the time what's in our shadow by what we judge, ridicule, and point out as flaws in other people. You know the old adage, "When you point one finger, there are three fingers pointing back at you." What we judge in another is indeed hidden in our very own shadow. If it wasn't in our shadow, we wouldn't find it so troublesome in other people.

When we reject an aspect of our self, however negative it appears, we also reject vital life energy and keep ourselves from full soul expression. Those so-called negative and undesirable traits contain crucial gifts that we need for wholeness. Let's go get them!

How do you get things out of your shadow?
This process can be rather fun after a while. Honest to goodness!

1. Recognize a judgment you have about someone.
2. We will use, "They are such an idiot!"
3. Imagine pulling 'idiot' out from behind you, out of your shadow, and gaze at it for a bit.
4. Then declare to yourself, "I can be an idiot. That is me. I recognize the idiot in me." This process is even more powerful if you can do it until you laugh about it all.
5. Find a few examples where it has indeed been true that you have been an idiot.
6. Find some benefit to having access to the energy of "idiot" (foolish, adventurous, unknowing, not enough, imperfection, unconscious behavior).

7. Send waves of love to that energy and embrace it as your own. Maybe even envision taking it into your heart and welcoming it with kindness and love.

I use this particular example because after doing this process for myself and embracing this idiot energy, my creativity and ability to write, paint, and produce artwork skyrocketed. It was now safe to be an idiot (foolish, imperfect), which is vital if you ever want to create anything. Another advantage was that I stopped judging it in others. Two huge benefits!

We are each the sum of everything in existence. When we can see, embrace, and love the light and shadow of everything and everyone within us, we free ourselves of judgment and open ourselves to fully express our beautiful nature.

Our shadows hold many amazing and precious gifts. I invite you to explore your treasures. Here are a few suggestions: bitch, ass, stingy, selfish, mean, narcissist, liar, terrorist, etc.

"When you embrace your shadow
you will no longer have to live in fear.
Find the gifts of your shadow and you will finally revel
in all the glory of your true self.
Then you will have the freedom to create the life
you have always desired."
~ Debbie Ford

RECOVERY

Things happen, negative worldviews are created, instincts are injured, and hearts are broken. Recovery is possible whether you have access to official resources of help or not. I know from my own recovery journey that the most important tool for recovery is desire—desire to heal wounds, desire for wellness, desire to find the real source of love and safety. This kind of desire (longing, craving, and yearning) needs to be a stubborn aspiration that no matter how long it takes, no matter what has to happen, no matter what it costs me emotionally, physically or spiritually, **I will be well!** Half-hearted attempts will fall far short of recovery.

Recovery truly begins when we are fed up, feel we have suffered enough, and we get hold of that stubborn determination and passion for being well.

How does one recover? My response to this question deserves its own book, which I hope to share with you one day. I can say, however, that each person's recovery is unique to the individual. No one else has the right to dictate how it's done, or limit what Love Itself will use to bring you forward one breath, one step at a time. Do not follow fear any longer. Let love be your guide. Follow only love and it will always lead you safely home.

> *"The goal of spiritual practice is full recovery,*
> *and the only thing you need to recover from*
> *is a fractured sense of self."*
> ~ Marianne Williamson

"The process of spotting fear and refusing to obey it
is the source of all true empowerment."
~ Martha Beck

INJURED INSTINCTS

Healthy instincts tell us what is right and good for us and what is a mistake. They tell us clearly when to run and when to stand up for ourselves or others. Injured instincts leave us in a state of confusion, where up is down, right is left, bullies are to be tolerated, and niceness is preyed upon by internal and external predators. Injured instincts lead us to all sorts of messy attempts to get love in all the wrong places.

Recovering healthy instincts is a vital part of living in a human body. Any attempts to bypass the healing process by becoming more spiritual will only delay your wellness. I highly recommend deeply exploring *Women Who Run with the Wolves* by Clarissa Pinkola Estés. Whether you are male or female, there are great riches to be found in the classic stories. This book transformed my life and brought me home to myself.

"Early training to 'be nice' causes us
to override our intuitions.
Imagine a wolf mom teaching her young to 'be nice'
in the face of an angry ferret or a wily snake."
~ Clarissa Pinkola Estés

HERE ARE A FEW IDEAS FOR REGAINING HEALTHY INSTINCTS:

1. First, admit that your instincts may be off kilter
   a. if you're a doormat and allow people to bully or control you
   b. if you invite people into your life that others can tell aren't good for you
   c. if you can't tell when it's time to peaceably leave a situation or job
   d. if you hold on after everyone else tells you to let go
   e. if your idea of love allows abuse
2. Find examples of healthy instincts and study them: including wild animal behavior, relatives, and admired public figures. Imagine stepping into them and trying on their way of being. How would they handle your situation?
3. Explore the difference between being nice and being kind.
   a. Being nice (good, pleasant) often holds the desire to be acceptable and safe; therefore it can come off as weak and manipulative, and is to a predator what a matador's cape is to a raging bull. Being nice invites bullies, aggression, and/or attack.
   b. Kindness can be thoughtful and benevolent, yet also allows room for empowerment, truth speaking, and no nonsense boundary setting. "This far, and no further!"
   c. Stop being nice to internal and external predators! And take "bitch" out of your shadow to embrace it fully. The energy of bitch won't make you mean. It will, however, give you full access to your power and wild wisdom.

4. Heal early wounds. Early wounds are any decisions and self-belittling stories (inner predator) that created a limited and disempowered worldview. It is good to have help with the healing process.
5. Find a loving companion who has permission to point out doormatish behavior.
6. Discover what true, unconditional love looks like, feels like, and acts like. Require others to treat you with that kind of loving respect. And you do the same for yourself and them.
7. Explore and practice non-violent communication.
8. From your new, higher perspective, create for yourself an affirming life story, of which you are the hero. Incorporate your wounds as the training for what you are here to do. They are a gift, after all.

"Good instincts usually tell you what to do before your head has figured it out."
Michael Burke

"Follow your instincts. That's where true wisdom manifests itself."
Oprah Winfrey

"Your mind knows only some things. Your inner voice, your instinct, knows everything. If you listen to what you know instinctively, it will always lead you down the right path."
Henry Winkler

*Intuition and instincts work better
when your mind filters are clean and clear.*
~ Marie Maguire

WHOSE FAULT IS IT?

Fault, mistake, blunder, liability—all of these words leave a heavy feeling of judgment and a dark burden of shame. How does fault finding benefit anyone? Fault finding is violent and unloving to say the least. What if we understood the behavior we label as a "fault" as a confused attempt to get love?

Everyone's foolish actions (faults) come from a confused attempt to get love. Sure, we might call it something else. We might call it a quest for power or safety, acceptance or belonging. No matter the words we use, they all lead back to our need and desire for love. We all want to be loved. Many of us are deeply confused about how to get that love. Our families and our culture often don't teach us how to get it in a healthy way. I know I was confused about how to get love in a healthy way!

Most television, movies, games, and books (current worldview) give us distorted ideas of what will satisfy our intense and driving need for love.

- A new relationship – even an unsanctioned one
- Ownership (car, house, clothes, jewelry…) – even if it has to be taken from someone else

- Membership – whether it's in a country club or a gang
- Win a fight – no holds barred, even with those who love us
- Sexual satisfaction – no matter who gets used or hurt
- New job – even if it strangles our soul
- Addictions – one more high will do it
- Violence and murder towards anyone who stands in the way – including your self

Each of these actions comes from a place of confusion. We are trying to get something that already belongs to us. The whole purpose of this life is to awaken from the confusion and discover the love that is already ours. We are loved. We are Love Itself. We have to get this love from inside of ourselves through connection with God. Love Itself is the only source of love that will ever truly satisfy.

So, when we (or someone else) do something from a place of confusion, don't waste time and vitality in the low energy of fault-finding and blame. Shake yourself off, have mercy, and get the help needed to find the real source of Love Itself.

"When you blame others, you give
up your power to change."
~ Robert Anthony

"When we attack others,
we must first denigrate the notion of
humanity within ourselves."

Empathy evaporates, leaving us free to
be verbally or physically violent.
There is a dear price to be paid in our soul,
for the fleeting pleasure of self-righteousness."
~ Unknown

"Teach me to feel another's woe, to hide the fault I see,
that mercy I to others show, that mercy show to me."
~ Alexander Pope

SEEING FROM A HIGHER PERSPECTIVE

As an artist, perspective is an important resource when creating a painting. I get to decide which point of view and which angle I'll use in presenting my chosen subject.

As a hiker of nature trails, my perspective changes depending on where I'm standing at any given moment. From the ground level perspective, I can see details of the trees and grass, and smell the sweet earthiness of the ground. Further along the trail and higher up, I'm able to see the winding pathway that led me there. If I took a helicopter ride over the same area I could see the trail from start to finish. This higher perspective would open my mind to all the things I might have missed when down at ground level.

As a spiritual explorer, perspective is even more valuable. When we're down on ground level we get enmeshed in the stories of life and talk about "what he did… they said… she is… how could they…?" When we get to higher ground, either because of the passing of years or an internal choice, we may see how what was said or done somehow worked out for us in an amazing fashion. When we've learned how to see from an even higher perspective (we've done the work of letting go of story, embraced our shadow and hugged our own confusions), we find so much awe and joy in knowing we've been safe, in Love Itself, all along.

I INVITE YOU TO PLAY WITH THIS HIGHER PERSPECTIVE:
Think of something you did as a small child for which you were punished or shamed. From your current adult perspective, you may allow yourself to see that yours was the action of an innocent and confused child. Allow yourself to feel compassion for that sweet younger you, and even imagine going back in time to help, hold, and comfort your younger self. Help the younger self to have a new understanding, so that he/she feels relieved and happy. Invite your younger self to relax in your arms with this new knowing. (You become the hero you've been waiting for.)

Now, envision a time in your future when you've grown in compassion and wisdom. Invite the future you to look upon the you of today with the same kind of compassion and comfort that you offered your younger self. Pour out the love and support you really need at this time. Be your own best friend.

Have your future wise self look back on a person whom you blame for something. See the event as if it had happened in the far distant past. Two hundred years will do for distance. I wonder if you can allow yourself to see the other person's actions, or words, as coming from their own confusion on how to get love? Your wise self may be able to let the blame and judgment go because you trust that in the higher scheme of things it turned out just right. It was all for learning and growing into your higher wise self. Forgive and express gratitude to the person for participating in your learning opportunity.

Seeing from a higher perspective is a powerful method of releasing blame, guilt, and shame, and it stops your suffering in its tracks. It produces forgiveness, compassion, and connection with Love Itself. To see from a higher perspective is to cut through the veils of ignorance, false appearance, projections, and internal story to see clearly that Love Itself surrounds you.

There will come a time, either in this life or in spirit form, when you can look back on this life and realize that everything was all right, and everything was woven together so perfectly by Love Itself. Why not take that view now and feel the joy? All is indeed well.

"From my perspective,
I absolutely believe in a greater spiritual power,
far greater than I am, from which I have derived strength
in moments of sadness or fear.
That's what I believe, and it was very,
very strong in the forest."
~ Jane Goodall

SEATING THE SOUL IN HIGHER AWARENESS

I imagine that most of us have noticed that we have a non-stop discussion going on inside our heads. This voice that we all hear talking inside us is the critical factor (or survival mind, or ego) that is an element of the physical brain. It may not surprise anyone that the main occupation of this voice is to discover "problems" (survival), create story about what it finds (meaning making), sort through solutions (swirling thoughts), inspire action to keep us safe, and then go on to find the next problem. Round and round it goes!

The good news, shared by Michael Singer in his book, *The Untethered Soul,* is that we are not that voice. We are the ones who hear the voice and observe its talking. If we pay attention to and believe everything that voice says, we could be in for a list of never ending problems! Problems are its specialty, and if it can't find some problems, it usually creates them because it does like to keep busy.

As we awaken to and truly desire emotional wellness and spiritual freedom, we may wish to understand that we are not the voice of the physical brain. We are the consciousness, the eternal soul who hears the voice. Hopefully, we will each come to see that the real cause of problems is not life (circumstances, challenges or people). The real cause of problems is the hullabaloo that the critical factor, the inner voice, makes about everything that happens. By becoming aware that you are the eternal soul that is listening to the voice and not the voice itself, spiritual awakening (and a much quieter mind) becomes available.

PROCESS FOR AWARENESS:

1. Become conscious of your breathing, especially the releasing of air.
2. Press your tongue to the roof of your mouth.
3. On one of the next exhales, allow your tongue to drop and let it settle easily and comfortably into your lower jaw.
4. As you exhale and drop your tongue, imagine that your soul, the eternal part of you, sits back into an imaginary seat; one where you are an eyewitness. This seat of higher awareness is a place from which you may listen and observe.
5. Allow your shoulders to drop, your jaw to relax, and your head to settle back.

People often describe a feeling of warm heaviness as they settle into this observer position. They also mention they feel more grounded, present in the moment, and much calmer. So, just to be clear, this is not dissociation (where one's consciousness goes for a hike while the body is still present.) No. When you settle into deeper awareness you are fully present and alert to all that transpires.

Here in this place, you are in the center of your consciousness. From this observer position you are aware of the thoughts, emotions, and experiences coming in through the body's senses. From here, when the voice speaks you can question its truth, comfort its fears, and silence the nonsense. This is the place of peace and spiritual awareness. This is also a great place to do inquiry or shadow work.

QUESTIONS FOR THE VOICE:

1. What are you afraid of? Talk to it and comfort it like it is a small child sitting on your lap, "There, there!"
2. What else is possible? This question helps our internal voice get out of the either/or thinking trap.
3. Really? Take the thought to a ridiculous point, until it makes you belly laugh.
4. What do you need to feel better? Careful here because the first answer is often full of fear and violence: "I need so-and-so to go away." A better, more empowered answer might be: "I notice that I prefer to spend this evening in quietness and solitude." The answer needs to be about you and not about others.

Example: I notice there is a feeling of anxiety swirling through me, so I seat my soul into this higher awareness. Once there, I see the anxiety as if it were a small child and have it sit on my lap for comfort. I listen to its fears, all the while holding it close and giving it the compassion it needs. Once it feels heard, it may be more willing to find a solution.

Example: I'm preparing to be in a meeting with someone who doesn't like, or approve of, me. I seat myself in this position of higher awareness, so that I'm fully present and yet not resisting, or running from, this person. It is a place of grounded neutrality like a sitting mountain. From this place I can listen, ask questions, maintain my personal space and stand firmly in what I know.

To explore more, I invite you to read *The Untethered Soul,* by Michael Singer.

EMPOWERED LIVING

Your parents weren't perfect. No parents are perfect. Your friends disappoint because they are human! Partners meet only some of your needs. People mess up in big and small ways because of confusion. If you feel anger about any of this, you are blaming others and not taking responsibility for yourself. When you blame others, your heart closes, energy is diminished, your power is given away, and there's not much left to hear inspiration and to take needed action.

It's easy to get stuck in "if only." If only my parents were more stable. If only my friends didn't disappoint me. If only my partner met more of my needs. If only my boss was more understanding. All of these thoughts give away your power.

Opening your mind, questioning your stories, waking up your awareness, expanding your heart, and growing spiritually are YOUR choices and your responsibility. Take empowered, open-hearted action. **Discover your need, and in a loving manner, give it to yourself.**

Old worldview

- My difficulties are everyone else's fault.
- I'm a victim of their bad behavior.
- If only everyone met my needs, like they should.
- Someone should come along and rescue me.

New worldview

- No matter what anyone else has said or done, I alone am responsible for myself.
- I give myself everything I need. (Warmth, love, compassion, affection, understanding, etc.)
- I empower myself and decide what comes next. I'm the one I've been waiting for.

> *"Nobody is responsible except you.*
> *Nobody can make you angry,*
> *and nobody can make you happy."*
> ~ Osho

> *"You are the one you've been waiting for."*
> ~ Unknown

LIFE/DEATH/LIFE CYCLE

Nature shows us, in glorious and inglorious ways, that there is a cycle to all aspects of our existence: seasons, relationships, reincarnation, and even within our own souls. There is an ebb and flow for all things under Heaven. This cycle is true of all experiences in this life and beyond, and when we resist the life/death/life cycle we miss out on a lot of great learning opportunities. There is a time to be born and times to die, and we, within our earth-bound consciousness, have no idea when those times are right. The best we can do is trust Love Itself to keep the ebb and flow moving in perfect rhythm. When we argue with what is, and declare that something ought to be different, we suffer. **As we wholeheartedly, trustfully embrace what is, then we have peace.**

EMBRACING WHAT IS (LOVE IS IN ALL OF IT)

- When someone is born it is time to be born.
- When one dies, whether 90 years old or nine minutes old, it is time to die.
- Relationships begin and end.
- Jobs begin and end.
- Health ebbs and flows.
- There are laughter and tears.

"For everything there is a season,
and a time for every matter under heaven:
a time to be born, and a time to die;

a time to plant, and a time to pluck up what is planted;
a time to kill, and a time to heal…"
~ Ecclesiastes 3:1–3

Embracing what is doesn't mean that we suppress emotions. Heavens no! Embrace what is, and let the energy of the emotions flow without judgment, without story, and without bitterness. **New life follows death as surely as spring follows winter.**

"We have been taught
that death is always followed by more death.
It is simply not so,
death is always in the process of incubating new life…"
~ Clarissa Pinkola Estés

PASSION AND CURIOSITY

Too often, we ignore our curiosity about particular topics or judge it as wrong. There is usually some fear-filled social or religious conditioning within us that warns us to stay away. Bad. Wrong. Selfish. Dangerous. Heretical. Old Fashioned. New Age. It takes a whole new level of trust to move forward against such warnings. Love Itself is the best touchstone for the journey of following our curiosity. We must learn to follow where inquisitiveness leads us, and give our trust to Love Itself to be our own personal guide to what is good and right for us as individuals.

As an avid reader and a perpetual student, I have found the right books, the right conversations, the right songs, and the right interests have jumped out in front of me at the right moment. What is right for me may not be right for you. Only you may decide. Only you know if what you are seeking is the power of love or the love of power. One will lead you home to Love Itself, and the other will lead to loads of confusion.

The places, practices, and topics that call to your soul are those that will most help you on this journey. Read that sentence again and again to fully understand the importance of following your curiosity. Your zeal for something may also be connected to other lives you've lived, bring a re-activation of soul gifts, talents, and skills polished in other incarnations, and may be useful for your time here as _____ (insert your name here).

You may have noticed that tarot, runes and astrology have been mentioned as great resources for the journey. Are they right for you? You have to trust that inner yes or no for the answer. Who knows, a no today could be a yes three years from now. Follow what is best for you and stay open and curious!

Old worldview

- Some tools and resources are bad or evil.

New worldview

- All tools and resources, when approached through love, are safe to explore.
- God will use a variety of tools to help me on my journey to living loved.
- It is safe to follow my curiosity, using love as a touchstone.

Our interests and desires are divinely inspired,
when filtered through, and focused toward, love.
~ Marie Maguire

WAYS TO CONNECT

When I was active in conservative religion there were many things that were considered out of bounds for "true" believers. Fear tactics were used to keep curiosity in check. In all of my explorations, including many topics labeled as New Age, I have found no evil. I have found unusual, outlandish, and seemingly off-balance people, ideas and things, yet I have found no evil.

1. Approaching any topic with a loving intent brings love into the endeavor. Love leads you into wisdom and clarity, and love is the outcome.
2. Approaching any topic, spirituality and religion included, with a desire for power or control over others, leads

into evil (confusion), and fear is the outcome (for self and others).

3. The heart is what matters, and love is the only sure guidepost.

I invite you to let love be your personal guide as you follow your curiosity and have fun exploring different ways for understanding yourself and others, as well as connecting with Love Itself. Here is a short list of wonderful tools for expanding your worldview. For getting started with many of these tools and practices, it is good to find a teacher you trust who is guided by love, and who, in return, respects you.

HELPFUL TOOLS

All styles of meditation, tarot, runes, astrology birth chart, numerology, north and south nodes, human design, hypnotherapy, shamanism, neurolinguistic programming (NLP), energy medicine, energy management, Reiki, Chi Gung, Jin Shin Jyutsu, past-life and natal regression, exploring intuition, meeting spirit animals and guides, messages from nature, Emotional Freedom Technique (EFT), Strengths Finder, temperament/personality types, and exploring the possibility of being gifted as a Highly Sensitive Person (HSP) or intuitive advisor.

"Respond to every call that excites your spirit."
~ Rumi

HELP IS ALWAYS AVAILABLE

"Ask, and it will be given to you; seek, and you will find; knock, and it will be opened to you."
~ Matthew 7:7 NIV

When you seek for help, you must seek with all of your heart. Half-heartedness will avail you nothing. What does whole-hearted seeking look like? It is stubbornly, persistently holding on to Love Itself no matter what trouble comes your way.

When we are halfhearted, we stop seeking when troubles come our way. Whole-heartedness (persistence) makes us much more determined in our actions and expectant for God to come through with the blessings. It is pushing through the troubles that helps us grow up, matures our beliefs, and proves our trust.

I've found hope when I wanted it, help when I asked and looked for it, and was shown love all along the way. It wasn't easy, and help didn't often look like what I expected. However, I've found Love to be ever faithful and compassionate. Even when the aid didn't happen as soon as I'd liked, then I learned to be still and trust that what was really needed (a most benevolent outcome) was on its way.

Example: In the midst of my dark night journey, it would have been easy to give up and collapse permanently into one of the many fear-based options presented to me. Instead, I held on to promises given to me along the way:

1. As great as the darkness has been so great shall be the light.
2. I will be found faithful to the end and plunder the enemy's camp (fear).
3. God is working all things out for my best and His purposes.
4. There is no roadmap to get me where I'm going.
5. Hold on, hold out. All will be well.

I created a Spiritual Biography that helped me keep my focus during the times of uncertainty and fear. In it I kept track of the comfort and help along the way. When I focused on these things, it was like being a horse with blinders on. The horse can only see what's directly ahead, and is unable to see the scary or distracting things in its side-line vision. I invite you to discover your spiritual truths, and put your blinders on, so that the spiritual truth is all you see. Keep moving forward toward Love Itself.

Example: One of my favorite stories of fun help being provided occurred many years ago. I was a young mother who had put together a wardrobe from delightful forays into second-hand stores and garage sales. I had everything I needed, except for new socks and belts. So, without mentioning the need to anyone else, I asked God for socks and belts, and left the need with Him. After a brief time, a good friend who was moving, asked me to come look at what she had available to give away. Grateful and skeptical, because my friend was much shorter than myself,

I went to be supportive, and we had a delightful visit. As I prepared to leave, she handed me a bag. "What's this?" I asked. "Well, I hope you don't mind, it's a collection of socks and belts I thought you might use," she replied. In the car, I burst out in laughing in gratitude for a God who cared about my desire for socks and belts. When I opened the bag, I discovered that the quality of the contents was far better than anything I could have purchased for myself.

Example: Money has been one of my great teachers in this life. I've had many opportunities to learn about trusting that "I'll have what I need, right when I need it." I've also had the occasion of being pushed, and judged, by those who think they know what I should be doing to fix my financial challenges. Every challenge, every judgment, every moment of trusting, has helped me refine my attitudes and faith and learn even more deeply that I'm always safe within Love Itself.

We are loved, I tell you.

> *God doesn't remove our challenges,*
> *He helps us through them.*
> ~ Marie Maguire

> *"You may encounter many defeats (yet),*
> *you must not be defeated.*
> *In fact, it may be necessary to encounter the defeats,*
> *so you can know who you are,*

What you can rise from, how you
can still come out of it."
~ Maya Angelou

AWARENESS SHIFT

Each shift in your awareness, every new belief added to your personal worldview, ripples out and changes every aspect of your experience (past, present and future).

Every shift affects the stories of the past and, if you let it, helps you to see them with a new and higher understanding. In fact, it is safe to say that **you have not fully embraced the new worldview until those old stories are transformed by the new knowing**. You cease suffering.

My old worldview said *tough luck* if you were sexually abused and acted out sexually on your road to recovery. This is sin. I am bad. I will be judged harshly for these repeated messed up actions.

My new worldview says I'm loved. My actions were based in confused attempts to get the love and safety I craved. I participated in planning the challenges I'd face with the intent of learning more about forgiveness and grace. Each lesson I learned would be used to console and assist others on their journey to Love. Love Itself cheered me on to get up again and again, falling into His joyous embrace.

EXAMPLES OF WORLDVIEW SHIFT (OLD=OLD WORLDVIEW / NEW=NEW WORLDVIEW)

Old: The world is not safe.
New: I am always safe, and love watches over me.

Old: I'm a victim and bad things happen to me because I'm bad (or they're bad).
New: I'm an empowered participant in the planning of this life, and learning opportunities are part of the plan.

Old: I have to take from others what I need (things, relationships, sex, power, "love").
New: I give to myself all that I need through healthy and loving ways.

Old: I'm not enough.
New: Everything I am and everything I need comes from the Source of all that is. I am all that I need for this journey as (insert your name).

Old: No one loves me / I'm unlovable.
New: I am loved and adored by the Beloved. I am part of Love Itself. I am love, so I deeply love myself! I give myself all the warmth and affection I need.

Some worldviews are easier to dislodge than others. When faced with a tough one, please seek out assistance for shifting those old beliefs that no longer serve you. Hypnotherapy and NLP are among the most powerful tools for healing early wounds and making permanent worldview changes.

"As a single footstep will not make a path on the earth,
so a single thought will not make
a pathway in the mind.
To make a deep physical path, we
walk again and again.
To make a deep mental path,
we must think over and over the kind of thoughts
we wish to dominate our lives."
~ Henry David Thoreau

THERE IS ONLY NOW

Some say that if you live in the past, you may feel depressed. If you live in the future, you may feel anxious. It is only in the *now* that help, hope, and peace are promised and available. When you feel anger, depression, anxiety, or fear, there is a really good chance (100%) you are not present in this moment and you are entangled in the past or future.

HOW DO YOU LIVE IN THIS MOMENT? HERE ARE SEVERAL DIFFERENT WAYS TO COME BACK INTO THIS MOMENT:

1. Follow your breath – counting on the exhale 36 breaths. If you lose count, start again.

2. Hold the Breath Hug – arms crossed with fingers in the arm pits, drop shoulders, breathe, and relax.
3. Bring awareness to your mid belly. Place your hand on your belly, "This is me in my body."
4. Walk barefoot out in nature, and bring full awareness into the experience.
5. Take notice of the texture of your clothes, or something nearby (chair, tree, keyboard).
6. Eat or drink mindfully, savoring every taste and texture.

BENEFITS OF LIVING IN THE NOW

When we are fully present in our bodies, in this moment:

- We have all we need.
- We can hear/feel inspired directions.
- Peace and love dwell in this moment.
- We are fully present for life experiences.
- We feel the organic flow of living.
- There are no shoulds, oughts or supposed-to's in the NOW
- We can feel the yes and no answers within our body.
- Inspiration and joy move us swiftly.
- We connect with Love Itself.

"I have realized that the past and
future are real illusions,
that they exist in the present,
which is what there is and all there is."
~ Alan Watts

"God introduces Himself as 'I am.'
He doesn't say, 'I was' (past), or 'I will be' (future).
He is the God of now, and all of His
love and promises of provision,
are available when we live in this moment."
~ Unknown

ALL MOMENTS ARE AVAILABLE NOW

Now is all there ever is, was, or will be. Scientists and philosophers are known to play around with the idea that all times, space, and dimensions are happening in this moment. Mind blowing!

In my experience as a hypnotherapist, I see, again and again, that all moments of the past, present, and future are available right now, and are therefore open to our creative healing intentions. I've found this to be a powerful tool in many a healing process.

I imagine we've all had conversations where we've said too much or too little. We remember situations where regret resides around actions taken, or missed, or parts of ourselves are still stuck in memories of suffering. I have good news! Every one of those moments, whether from this life or another, is available right here, right now, for empowerment and healing.

1. As a child, on the playground, I walked up to a group of girls, and one turned and said, "We don't want you!" This statement fit right in with my old worldview that I was unlovable. Even though her eyes told me that she was trying to be funny, I interpreted her humor as rejection aimed at me. Taking it personally, I walked away in love-less despair.

   a. Using my imagination, I took my adult self back to that moment, so that when my child self turned away, she walked right into my adult arms. We strolled around the playground, and talked. I helped her have a new under-standing, and even a love for herself, so when she felt full and ready I escorted her back to that moment where she joined in and laughed with them over the event.

2. Some traumatic events occurred before I ever had lan-guage or ability to defend myself.

   a. I took my adult self back into the original event, and this time the adult part of me spoke up on behalf of that sweet, innocent little girl and created a different outcome.

3. Early in my adult life, I wasn't always so good at commu-nicating my thoughts and needs.

   a. I went back and endowed my younger adult self with better resources, and let her have many new (more empowered) conversations with family, friends, lov-ers, children, and herself.

4. In a past life, I was forced into the convent by a father who was angry that I wouldn't marry the man chosen for me. There was much anger, regret, and disillusionment.

   a. My current self met that past-life self in the inter-life to explain how things work, and explore how she could communicate, and make an empowered bargain with her father. She chose to go back into that life before this event ever occurred, and developed a better and more open relationship with her father. She got him to agree that if she didn't marry by the age of twenty, she herself would choose to enter the convent. By the time she reached the assigned age, she was ready and willing to enter spiritual service, and her father was now reluctant to let her go. She, feeling called rather than forced, went into the convent with great joy and peace.

How does this work? All of our memories are stored in a kind of mind movie. When we sit in a meditative state, in our imagination we can go back and change, rearrange, and redo those scenes. The changes to the mind movie then changes how our body and emotions respond in the now. Healing those past events empowers our current self to be even more present, peaceful and loved, right now.

Does it change the original event? If it changes how you feel in the now, does it even matter?

I'm curious how you will benefit from exploring these ideas.

"The past, the present and the future
are really one: they are today."
~ Harriet Beecher Stowe

PATH TO HAPPINESS

Happiness can be an elusive thing. If only ... If only I had more money, *then* I'd be happy. If I had a better job, better health... the list goes on and on. Even when we do happen to achieve one of those goals, happiness stays only a fleeting moment. It is there until our problem-focused mind (critical factor) discovers only one more thing that must change before happiness becomes permanent. Even so, there are happy people who don't have any of those things we might list as necessities for happiness. What is their secret? Gratitude.

GRATITUDE IS THE MOST POWERFUL PATH TO HAPPINESS. HERE ARE SOME WAYS TO PRACTICE GRATITUDE:

- Create a daily gratitude habit, and include your body, head to toes. Also include challenges and learning opportunities.
- Have fun and laughter every single day. Remember how to play and then go do it!
- Spread the appreciation to others through notes, email, text, phone calls and other creative ways.

- Show your open-hearted thanks in your eyes as you smile at others.
- Rejoice always, trusting that everything (every: thing, person, event, heartache, challenge, and so on) that comes your way comes through Love Itself, and will produce a benevolent outcome.
- Begin and end each day with heartfelt, smiling thankfulness.

Let gratitude become a state of being that fills your way of life. I imagine you will be amazed and delighted at the results. You may even discover that you are happier than ever before.

Old worldview

- I must have what I want to be happy.
- Happiness is a gift bestowed by the gods.
- Happiness depends on being free of karmic debt.

New worldview

- Happiness is a choice.
- Gratitude is a path to happiness.
- Everything that comes my way is an invitation to be grateful.
- I choose to trust and be thankful.

This moment calls for gratitude
and more and more gratitude.
~ Marie Maguire

"The greatest thing is to give thanks for everything.
He who has learned this knows what it means to live."
~ Albert Schweitzer

BLESS EVERYTHING AND EVERYONE
Bless—make holy, approve of.

I am spirit. I bless each and every one of us and invite each of us to wake up to the incredible power and love of spirit that flows through everything with great passion, grand intention, and peace. Awaken and arise all you people, celebrate life, and vibrate at the speed of love, and we shall have peace.

1. Your job is to wake up and bless the world and everything in it. "Blessed be …"
2. Blessing is inconceivably powerful and is perhaps the greatest tool of all, because it is the direct pathway back to spirit.
3. Blessing is the act of recognizing, acknowledging, and saying *yes* to Love's action in your life, even if you don't understand the surface story.
4. It is nearly impossible to bless if you have no gratitude and have not forgiven yourself or others.
5. When you are able to bless, you feel more expansive, more powerful, happier, more connected, and you see all things clearly.

Old worldview

- Curse those who have cursed me.
- Do harm to those who have harmed me.

New worldview

- Stay physically safe, and bless those who curse me.
- Be thankful for all things. It shows I believe that Love Itself is guiding me.
- Celebrate life and bless everyone.

Blessed be my neighbors; each and every one,
Blessed be my "enemy"; might harmony truly come,
Blessed by my friends; may I serve with an open heart,
Blessed be my world; and let peace - within me - start.
~ Marie Maguire

GOD'S PATIENCE

God already knows how many tries it takes to get past a troubling life challenge and waits with joy for your freedom. Let's say that God knows that it will take you thirty-seven times to be delivered from a "sinful" (read: confused action) challenge. When you do it for the tenth time, His response is not anger, impatience, or a cutting remark like, "There he/she goes again! What is wrong with him/her?" No. Your Loving Father/Merciful Mother says, "Wahoo!

Only twenty-seven more times to go." Whether it takes you five minutes or five lifetimes, you will get there at last and at the right moment. You are surrounded and guided by love every step of the way.

Old worldview

- God is impatient.
- God will punish my feeble attempts.
- I get only so many tries to get past this challenge.

New worldview

- I'm loved and celebrated.
- It is safe to try again and again and again.
- God knows how long it will take me to learn something.
- Love Itself celebrates every step of my journey.
- Love cheers me on and holds me close.

"The lump of clay,
from the moment it comes under the
transforming hand of the potter,
is, during each day and each hour of the process,
just what the potter wants it to be at that
hour or on that day [or that life]
and therefore pleases him...
God's works are perfect in every stage of their growth."
~ Hannah Whitall Smith

THINKING CAN GET IN THE WAY OF KNOWING

Our left-brain thinking processes are influenced by our experiences, education, and cultural programming (our worldview), which, if you've been paying attention, makes the content of our thoughts rather suspect, to say the least. Our worldview influences the track followed by our analytical process, so thoughts can be true within our worldview and untrue elsewhere. Do you want new and truer thoughts? Change your worldview.

"Birds born in a cage think flying is an illness," says Alejandro Jodorowsky. There is no room within the caged bird's worldview for freedom or flight. In the same way, your thoughts may go round and round on an analytical search for absolute knowledge, demanding proof and certitude before accepting anything as true. Yet, all this thinking is taking place within a worldview with no room for "freedom or flight." Moreover, as Einstein, the archetype for genius, says, "We cannot solve our problems with the same thinking we used when we created them."

All of this left-brain analysis can get in the way of knowing, and may keep one stuck in a swirling circle of non-belief and non-action. Let us open to what else is possible!?

There is another side of the mind. It's one that more easily embraces the mysteries of life, and it doesn't demand the same level of proof. It embraces visceral experience. It trusts gut reaction. It honors spiritual connection. Take that step to the right side of your brain, and you'll soon discover that **certainty is an illusion**. I realize this idea may frighten some of you, yet I request that you hold on, and keep reading.

Even though the right side of the mind is also influenced by our worldview, it holds the keys to creativity, intuition, emotion, inter-personal connection, faith, and spirituality. These are invaluable tools that help us embrace a wider and more loving worldview. To access it means deciding to respect and value its own unique styles of knowing.

It may not be able to give rational explanation; however, there is a deep knowing, which when acted upon, saves you time and suffering. It's that gut feeling that sometimes has to shout, and may even create physical illness, to get your attention. Valuing intuitive knowing may require a leap of faith, at least at the beginning. From my experience, it is well worth the leap.

The intuitive, creative right brain speaks to us through feelings of yearning, passions, gut instincts, physical symptoms, dreams, visions, and flashes of what is right and best. We can more easily access the riches of the right brain flow through these multi-sensory activities:

- Movement, dance, gardening, flowing water
- Running, walking, any outdoor activity
- Creativity, play, color, getting messy
- Art, poetry, music, singing, meditation
- Imagination, pretending, daydreaming

ONE THING TO BE AWARE OF:
IF this right-brain knowing comes with strong emotion attached, it's a good bet the information you're receiving rico-
cheted around an off-kilter worldview that is in need of healing.
There is work to be done to clear your filters or replace your
lens.

Little, or no, emotion? Then you may trust you've got a
clear lens, and it's safe and sound to act on the information.
If this information leads you to expanding your heart, mind
or worldview, then know that any fear that presents itself
will fall like a paper wall when approached by living loved
techniques.

We need both sides of the mind, so if you respect one side
more than the other, you're lopsided and missing out on rich
resources intended to balance your life. If you, after all of your
attempts, personally have access to only one side of your brain,
find a trusted advisor who can share with you the invaluable
resources of the other side.

I highly recommend reading *My Stroke of Insight* by Jill Bolte
Taylor. At the very least, please watch her TED Talk by the same
title.

> *"The intuitive mind is a sacred gift;*
> *the rational mind is a faithful servant.*
> *We have created a society that honors the servant*
> *and has forgotten the gift."*
> ~ Albert Einstein

"What we don't know may present itself
as we loosen our grip on what we think we do know."
~ Robert Mann

Beware! Respecting the right side of the mind
may take you off the beaten path,
may require you embrace and
unleash your authentic self,
and may even cause you to be misunderstood.
All with your best interest at heart, of course.
~ Marie Maguire

KNOWING – THAT MAKES A DIFFERENCE

We seem to live in a world that has acquired the habit of collecting information and not acting on it. Using the ideas in this book as an example, let's say you read through the entire book, store the information in your head, and go right on suffering. "I know that already, and it hasn't made a bit of difference!" you say with irritation. You have the information and yet it doesn't do you any good. It's been stockpiled into your brain and hasn't made the transition into the kind of knowing that is stored in your bones and lived out in daily life.

Really knowing something, so that it transforms your worldview, comes from allowing ideas to make the twelve-inch journey from your head down into your heart. This drop down into your heart connects you to your spiritual and physical bones.

So, how does one make the leap from thinking about an idea to knowing it? Each of us might do this next step a little differently; nevertheless, the general idea is to embrace worldview expansion by first saying a resounding, "Yes!" to change.

- Choose a topic.
- Read it again and again.
- Meditate on all the different aspects.
- Journal your thoughts and feelings.
- Talk to your soul friends about it.
- Create a collage, a dance, or act it out.
- Imagine how acting on the idea will change how you live.
- Pretend you believe it and act *as if* it were true for you – until it is!
- Daydream about what your life looks like when you're living loved.
- Create a mantra that is repeated until it becomes first nature.
- Tell yourself the new worldview story over and over.
- Do the things you'll do when you really believe it.
- Find your own unique way of embracing Love Itself.

Do some or each of these until you feel the hope and love flood your soul.

This worldview changing process doesn't always happen in five minutes! Whether it takes minutes, months, or millennia, take all the time you need, for it is time well invested for a peace and love filled life.

Example: Years ago, I was driving over to visit a friend who lived on a farm 20 miles away. Before leaving home, I had a sudden idea to bring toilet paper with us. I thought (analytical left brain) this silly, and couldn't imagine myself walking up to the door with TP under my arm. So, I didn't. Thirty minutes into our visit one of the children needed to use the facilities, and my friend apologized saying they didn't have any toilet paper. I told her my story, packed everyone in the car, drove back to my home (there was no store close by) and retrieved the toilet paper. The extra 40 miles of travel was to instill this experience into my memory, so that next time I would listen to that intuitive knowing (right brain). It worked.

Example: I once was a client for another hypnotherapist, because asthma suddenly returned to me after years of silence. It kept acting up and making life miserable. We did a process to discover what message the asthma was trying to bring to conscious awareness. My body was upset with me for not taking care of myself, and it gave specific examples. My thoughts and worries about what others would think kept me from acting in my own best interest. Once this message was delivered, the asthma agreed to stop "shouting" as long as I promised to act on the new information. I agreed, and have not had trouble since. Knowing how to take care of one's self and doing it are two different things.

I've had many conversations with friends and clients, where an idea is presented, and the response is, "I know that," yet it's clear that the knowing in the head has not made the journey down into the heart and bones, where it would inspire action and peace of mind. We, each of us, have had this experience.

What idea is firmly in your head and wants to drop down into the knowing that inspires peace? Which topic in this book will you meditate on first? What will life be like when you pay attention to, and partner with, your body when it tells you what it knows? How much healthier and happier might you be? What "leap of faith" is calling to you? How will life be different when you choose to live loved?

> "Doubt kills more dreams than failure ever will."
> ~ Shel Silverstein

> As we honor intuitive knowledge by taking action,
> our subconscious becomes aware we are listening,
> and tells us more.
> ~ Marie Maguire

FROM CERTAINTY TO UNKNOWING
It's funny how much of our life leads us to gain knowledge, and then when we have it, we may be led to let it go and not know anything for sure. This "not-knowing" is a deeply wise place to be.

CERTAINTY

The critical factor of our physical brain loves to figure things out. It works hard at becoming absolutely sure, and puts that knowledge into neat little boxes based on duality: black/white, either/or, right/wrong, good/bad, saint/devil, love/hate, healthy/sick, empathic/narcissist, etc. It has good intentions as it wants to keep us safe; however, the resulting certitude closes us off from love and curiosity, and keeps us stuck in a spiral of negative judgments or confused actions.

We live in a far more multifaceted (think of the beauty of gemstones) and full color world. The spiritual journey invites us to move beyond dualistic thinking and open to other possibilities; to see what else is possible. Let go of certitude. Have an "I don't know anything!" curiosity and investigate what else is possible; for there is joy and freedom in unknowing everything!

UNKNOWING

Hopefully our certitude will wear itself out, we will tire of the black/white thinking and harsh judgments, and will allow ourselves to come full circle to the place of unknowing. **When we think we know what THE truth is, we don't yet know anything.** The place of unknowing is a deeply spiritual place of being comfortable with not having a clue about anything and allowing everyone else to journey in a way that makes sense to them.

EXAMPLES:

- I used to be certain there was only one way to God. Now, I've no idea and I'm at peace with the not knowing! However, I suspect that God will travel any path to find us.
- I used to be sure that when others didn't like or understand me, that it was because they were bad, evil, no-good, and so on (or I was). Now, I realize that I've no idea who they really are, and that their reaction has everything to do with them and nothing to do with me.
- I used to gather up as much knowledge as possible, thinking that if I understood better, that everything would make sense and I'd cease to suffer. I became certain about a lot of things, and rather ignorant of what really mattered - Love. Love wishes to disintegrate all barriers.
- I was certain that if you didn't do things (dishes, vacuuming, relationships, conversations, faith, etc.) my way that you were wrong. Ha! How silly we can be.
- I was certain that my way of being in the world was the only right way. When I opened to other possibilities the world became a wondrous and curious place.

Old worldview

- There is only one right way.
- It is possible to know something with certainty.

New worldview

- I don't know anything for sure, and that's okay.
- Because of love, I'm safe within the mystery that is life.

> *"I want to know . . .*
> *Then, a knowing that is unknowable,*
> *Speaks to me in a voice imperceptible,*
> *And discernible only in Spirit;*
> *It lovingly explains to me . . .*
> *. . .That part which seeks to know,*
> *Is part of the illusion . . ."*
> ~ Francine Collier

INNOCENCE

We are all as innocent and as guiltless as the child born yesterday. Our fumbling and confused actions are only a child's desperate attempt to find its way home to Love Itself. When we discover and embrace this innocence for ourselves, we're able to embrace it in others. **All of us are innocent.** Meditate on this thought and draw on it as a mantra prayer, to bring it deeply into your being. The only real remedy for guilt and shame is to embrace the innocence that comes with connection to Love Itself. Love is enough.

"I am innocent. You are innocent. We may have been confused, yet we are innocent. I am part of you, you are part of me. Blessed be our innocence."

Old worldview

- We are all guilty.
- We are born guilty.
- Shame is our natural feeling state.

New worldview

- We are all innocent.
- I am innocent.
- All confused actions are an attempt to get love and safety.
- I may be confused yet I'm still innocent.
- All of my enemies are innocent as well.

> *"There is so much good in the worst of us,*
> *And so much bad in the best of us,*
> *That it hardly behooves any of us*
> *To talk about [judge, label, reject, hate] the rest of us."*
> ~ Edward Wallis Hoch

Questioner: How are we to treat others?
Ramana Maharshi: There are no others.

MIRRORS

Mirrors are a useful tool for getting egg off our face, straightening clothes, and checking our emotional state by the look on our face. They give us the opportunity to see ourselves clearly and make adjustments to how we present in public. We appreciate their usefulness. People and circumstances offer the same practical tool for seeing ourselves clearly. Although, it's a bit trickier to see ourselves in these "mirrors," because we so want what we see to be about "them" and not us. How do human mirrors work?

I'm an INFJ, the rarest personality type and therefore the least known or understood. All through my life people have projected their judgments onto me, telling me who I am or who I'm not. This was confusing because it was often different from what I knew, so I'd question and berate myself for being "that". As I did more internal work to heal wounds, grew into a sense of myself and developed healthy boundaries, I finally discovered that people were really telling me who they were. It wasn't me they were seeing – it was them! The clearer I got, the easier it was to tell when they were projecting themselves onto my mirror. "You are so vindictive!" Nope. "You are lazy!" Nope. "You are unstable!" Ehh, nope. Certainly I check every label cast at me to see if there is shadow work to be done to reclaim a part of myself. I get clear, and then know what I need to say or do to handle it. Now, mostly, I let people have their mirror judgments. Maybe they are useful? Maybe it doesn't matter? Maybe they need it for their own growth journey?

As you're going through life there are bound to be incidents where you're triggered by what you see in a human mirror. If you're in any kind of relationship with humans, you'll get triggered. When you have a strong emotional reaction or negative judgment, that you assume is inspired by that person, there is (always) a mirror reflecting back aspects of yourself. This is an important opportunity! Don't let it pass you by, for how you respond means you get to reclaim, or reject, parts of yourself over and over again.

GENERAL EXAMPLES:

- Your partner is home all day raising kids, doing laundry, cooking and cleaning. You walk in and the only thing you notice is that the sink is full of dishes, and you call the partner, "Lazy!" It just might be you that is lazy.
- You're uncertain you made the right decision to marry and have wandering eyes, yet it's your loving partner that you repeatedly accuse of being unfaithful.
- You have a busy job running several programs, yet you're so organized that your office and desk are clean. Your boss sees this clean office and accuses you of not doing anything. The whole office knows it's the other way around. You are his mirror.
- The Pastor rages from the pulpit about child abuse and has the church gang up on a member who is struggling with that issue. You can bet that the Pastor is also overusing power with his own family.
- You have a conversation where you're sure you understand the agreement. You do the agreed upon thing and

discover you got it wrong. You get accused of being vindictive. The other is certain you didn't misunderstand;
you did it on purpose to punish them, so they threaten to
punish you. They are the one who is being vindictive and
projecting it on to you.

When you react to others with negative projections, and
therefore have neither compassion nor mercy for others, you
hate something about yourself. When you choose to embrace,
honor, and celebrate every aspect of your being, you become
a whole and complete soul. When you recognize your mirror projections, you can bring your shadow into the light and
say "I am that!" With kindness and compassion for yourself
(and then the other), you become love itself and your mirror
is clear. This kind of wholeness gives you access to your full
energy, wellness, and empowered soul. When you are seeing yourself and others this clearly, it is simple to make wise
decisions.

It also works the other way around! When you admire an
aspect about another person or see the beauty and radiance of
their being, it is only a reflection of something already alive and
active inside of you, that you have yet to celebrate. "I am that!"
Embrace your light and allow it to shine.

MAKING RELATIONSHIP DECISIONS
How do you know when you need to stay in a situation
and work on yourself (mirror work)? Or, when it is best to
leave?

In a relationship, when you experience negative emotional reactions, express internal or external judgments, or feel like you would "never do such a thing," there is internal work to be done to heal your own stuff. This person or situation is offering you a gift to help you heal yourself. This is, of course, assuming you are physically and emotionally safe. If you're not safe, move on and do the healing inner work from a distance. Be sure to know, however, that spirit may present you with other similar mirrors until the work is completed.

When you've done your inner work, and you see something in another and maintain a calm, loving, and nonjudgmental demeanor, you may be seeing clearly. You may also be clear enough to hear Spirit concerning whether it is more loving and wise to create distance, or if it is best to stay close and participate in their journey. Love Itself knows what is best. There is no right or wrong answer and Love Itself will support you either way.

I've found it helpful to journal my way through such decisions. What have I gained or learned from this person/situation? Ways I've benefited? What do I need? What I can give to myself? What I'd miss? What I won't miss? Which option feels even a tiny bit better in my heart? And any other questions that need answering. Usually, my way forward becomes clear and I feel empowered to take action.

Mirror and shadow work are quite related. The mirror is how we learn to see ourselves and shadow work is taking our rejected aspects out of the darkness to heal and embrace them.

"In this holographic world, everyone
and everything is a mirror,
and you are always seeing yourself
and talking to yourself.
If you choose, you can now look at what
emotionally affects you as an alarm,
a catalyst for growth that gives you an opportunity
to reclaim a hidden aspect of yourself."
~ Debbie Ford

"The world is a looking-glass,
and gives back to every man the
reflection of his own face."
~ William Makepeace Thackeray

We do not see, or know anything,
beyond our own level of perception.
I can know you only insofar as I know myself,
even then I better check in with
you to see if it's accurate.
~ Marie Maguire

WHOSE SPIRITUAL PATH IS RIGHT?
Countless wars have been fought over this question of which religion is right. We have taken turns terrorizing one another trying to prove who is right. I have heard the many sides of this

discussion. One is where debate is used to prove which spiritual path is correct. And another group says that all paths lead to the same place. This debate is a good example of either/or thinking. I invite you to consider another possibility; that **the paths themselves have no meaning at all, except what we give them.** The meaning comes from our own personal worldview!

So, let's say that I'm journeying along, and for a time I'm Catholic. There are great riches to be found in this path, and I am delighted for a time. After awhile, I feel restless and unsatisfied, so I move on to another path that intrigues me. Again there is delight for a time, and then dissatisfaction or curiosity may set in. Of course, being human, the path I left becomes wrong/foolish/evil, and the newly discovered path becomes the only way to God. Some of us keep doing this embrace and release process over and over, thinking that we are on the search for the perfect belief system that will get us to Heaven, and answer our needs.

The path, the religion, the system, the law (rule), the process, is not the "thing" that matters. Relationship is what matters. **In and of themselves, all religious and spiritual paths lead nowhere. However, God will travel any path to find you.** Love Itself loves you and will meet you wherever you are! As you fully embrace that knowing, a joyous freedom will arise inside your soul!

Your relationship with God, internal and external, is what matters. The form of belief or worship is not what matters. Love invites us to find our own way into relationship with Spirit. As you truly take this new worldview into your soul, only then are you free to travel any path that suits your unique being and connection to God, and are able to give that same freedom to others.

Old worldview

- There is only one right way to God.
- There is a perfect belief system and I must find it.
- Or, all paths lead to God.

New worldview

- All paths lead nowhere in particular.
- God will travel any path to find me.
- I'm safe to travel any path that inspires me.
- Love will lead me safely home.

"True love never forces."
~ Wm. Paul Young

"I will not glory, even in my orthodoxy,
for even that can be a snare if I make a god of it...
Let us rejoice in Him in all His
fullness and in Him alone."
~ D. Martyn Lloyd-Jones

WE ARE SAFE TO SEARCH, QUESTION, AND EXPLORE

Each of us has a unique relationship with God/Father/Mother/Source. Relationship with God is not one-size-fits-all.

If you've ever had, or even known, several children, you're aware that each is unique, and what inspires one, repels another, what discipline works for one, depresses the other. One needs structure, while another needs freedom. One craves warm affection, while another avoids touch. One loves math and science, while another delights in music and language. Need we go on?

If we, as human parents, give what we are best able to give our children according to their own unique needs; how much more does our Heavenly Father/Mother give to each of us?

There is no one right way for each of us to journey to Love Itself. We must each follow our unique needs, passions, and curiosities, in our journey to love. We must search, question, and explore the paths that seem best in our eyes, and Love Itself will find us on our own unique path. Let only love inspire us to move on to the next learning.

> *"Does that mean," asked Mack, "that*
> *all roads will lead to you?"*
> *"Not at all," smiled Jesus...*
> *"Most roads don't lead anywhere.*

*What it does mean is that I will
travel any road to find you."*
~ Wm. Paul Young

WE ARE NOT THIS BODY

We are not the body that we inhabit; neither are we this gender, race or nationality. We are eternal souls who inhabit a body. We choose to come here again and again to have fun and to grow. Everything we experience is fertile ground for great good, designed especially for us. All is for joy and/or learning! Choose to let it be both.

IMAGINE YOURSELF BELIEVING THESE THOUGHTS. WHAT WOULD CHANGE? WHAT WOULD HEAL?

1. This body is not me. Yet, I get to learn a lot about living fully in this body.
2. I live this life as _____ with a certain gender, personality, body type, race, religious tradition, etc. They are not me!
3. I am the eternal soul who inhabits this body and experiences the challenges of this life.
4. I may choose to accept it or reject it. However, it is just right for me this time around.

5. I may choose to come here again in a different body, with a new gender and personality, etc. to enjoy other challenges.
6. I may have other children, spouses, "enemies" and challenges.
7. I am so much more than I currently see or know, and so is everyone else!

Old worldview

- I am this body (gender, race, etc.) and I'm stuck with it.
- I'm a victim of chance.

New worldview

- I chose the challenge of living in this body / this life.
- This life is perfect for the things I'm hoping to learn.
- It is all for fun and for learning.
- Our souls are far more, and greater than, the roles we play in this life.

"Humans don't usually get to experience
the full magnificence of their lives
while they're living it. They get
caught up in lots of ideas
and lose sight of the miracle that is their life."
~ Annie Kagan

THANKFULNESS

Gratitude, rejoicing, and thankfulness are the most life-giving response to everyday life and show that we trust Love Itself. Grumbling and complaining are the opposite and show that we don't trust that we are loved and safe.

Gratitude will ease your journey. Every moment of your life is as it ought to be. To think otherwise produces insanity and suffering. Everything happens to you, and for you, at the right moment. When you respond AS IF you've chosen IT (current life circumstances), you are empowered by Love, rather than chased by fear. Rejoice for each and every moment, trusting that Love Itself causes all things to work together for your best and highest good. Trust in love.

I've lived in many places and the one topic I hear the most grumbling about is the weather. No matter whether it's sunny, cloudy, dry or wet, it is invariably the wrong weather desired. This grumbling habit seems like such a small thing, yet I've observed it making people miserable over something that is way beyond anyone's control. What would life be like if you acted AS IF you've chosen the weather and have fun with what is presented to you? What if you trust the weather patterns to Love Itself and go about your life delighted with the beauty that surrounds you? If you were planning on a walk and it starts to rain, put on your galoshes and jump in the puddles!

Joy and misery are in your hands, and thankfulness turns you toward one and away from the other.

*"There is not one blade of grass, there
is no color in this world
that is not intended to make us rejoice."*
~ John Calvin

*"Rejoice always ... give thanks in all circumstances;
for this is the will of God in Christ Jesus for you."*
~ I Thessalonians 5:16-18

LEARNING OPPORTUNITIES

A learning opportunity is any difficult life challenge related to jobs, relationships, birth, death, loss, illness, etc. Resistance to a learning opportunity is pointless, since these will be presented to us in various forms until we have learned whatever it is we planned to learn. All parts of life contain learning opportunities. If we are alive, there are things to be learned.

What are we generally setting ourselves up to learn? It is all about love! Kindness, patience, mercy, grace, gentleness, forgiveness, how to communicate without harming ourselves or others, how to keep our hearts open, how to embrace the full light of love, seeing with clear vision uncluttered by our own mythical stories, authenticity... You get the idea.

Don't like this idea? You'd prefer an easier life? You believe that life should be smooth and easy. As stated earlier in this book, that worldview that is the perfect set up for misery! **If**

you choose to change only one of your worldview beliefs, let this be the one! Embracing life as a fun adventure, full of wild and crazy learning opportunities, will make all the difference in your life.

The path to love is to trust that every learning opportunity comes directly from Love Itself. When you act AS IF you chose it, and plan to cooperate with it, you will have more peace in your life. Love Itself has good intentions for you, and offers help for facing every opportunity. You are safe and you are loved! You may find it helpful, when facing any challenge, to tell yourself, "this path is a perfect set up to learn about patience (forgiveness, kindness, nonviolent communication, etc.) This worldview will focus your heart and mind to participate more fully in the process, and guide you to ask clearly for the help that is needed.

Old worldview

- Life should be easy and there's something wrong if it isn't.

New worldview

- Life is a wild and crazy adventure, full of learning opportunities.

Expect obstacles and face them head on.
They are going to come up so the way you handle them
is what makes all the difference.
~ Lance Dale

*"When everything seems to be going against you,
remember that the airplane takes off
against the wind, not with it."*
~ Henry Ford

*The true measure of a man is not how he behaves
in moments of comfort and convenience
but how he stands at times of
controversy and challenges."*
~ Martin Luther King Jr.

THOUGHTS ON DEATH

Death is only a doorway back to the "other side" of home. This transition is a sacred passage as wondrous as birth, and is to be celebrated as such. When we are done doing and learning, whatever we decided to do and learn, it's time to "die" or transition home. Whether we live here 90 years or nine minutes, it is just right. Who are we to say otherwise? To say that someone has died too soon creates an insanity in us that produces loads of unnecessary suffering.

When you really believe that you are loved, you're always safe. Even in the dying process, you're safe. Your loved ones are safe. Help will be given to ease the journey. When loved ones die, you are always together, and you will be together again and again.

Meditate on this section until you incorporate it into a new worldview.

Old worldview

- Death is the worst thing that can happen.
- Death is a form of punishment.
- People should live a long time.
- No one should die young. It's a tragedy to die young.

New worldview

- Death is a transition back to the other side of home.
- Birth is a transition to this side of home.
- Each happens at just the right moment.
- I am always safe and guided, even in transition.
- I'll see my loved ones again and again.
- Here is no better than there. There is no better than here. All is Love Itself.
- All is well and all will be well.

"The fear of death follows from the fear of life.
A man who lives fully is prepared to die at any time."
~ Mark Twain

"I believe there are two sides to the
phenomenon known as death,
this side where we live, and the other side
where we shall continue to live.

Eternity does not start with death.
We are in eternity now."
~ Norman Vincent Peale

'There' is no better than 'here'.
Each is an important part of 'home'.
When we long for there so much
that we cease being here,
we are out of balance and wholeness. We are confused.
~ Marie Maguire

WHAT IS THE GENERAL PLAN FOR THIS LIFE?

Your general life plan is to remember that you are a spiritual being, that you are love, and that this life as (insert your name) is a dream for the purpose of joy and learning.

Your specific life plan, whether the audience is large or small, is evidenced by the things that challenge you: being completely yourself, living healthfully in the body, becoming a whole/healed person, taking care of the earth/animals/nature, communication, compassion, care-giving, mercy, forgiveness, teaching (the list is truly endless). And your greatest challenges become the gifts that you bring the world in your own unique way.

Example: In my life I've been given opportunities to lose and regain my voice, to fall repeatedly to learn humility and mercy, and to be inundated by fear, so I'd be inspired to search for and find Love Itself. Communication has been my chief challenge because it is the gift I'm here to bring this time around.

We choose to come back here again and again; to play other roles, face new challenges, and bring timely gifts; all as we grow on our soul's journey.

"If life gets too hard to stand, kneel"
~ Gordon Hinckley

"Do something today that your future
self will thank you for."
~ Unknown

"He has shown you, O man, what is good;
and what does the LORD require of you
but to do justly, to love mercy, and to
walk humbly with your God?"
~ Micah 6:8 (NKJV)

OUR SOUL'S HIGHER PLAN

Prior to birth, what if you have in-depth conversations with your guides, spiritual advisers, and the other souls with whom you will share your coming incarnation. You may discuss the lessons you hope to learn, and the ways in which you may learn them. Regardless of the specific challenges a life contains, every plan is based on love. Each soul in the plan is motivated by the desire to give and receive love, and to help each other reach goals. Even in the instances when a soul has agreed to play a "negative" role to stimulate another's growth, the plan is inspired by love.

One does not have to believe in this concept to benefit from it. I ask only that you consider: What if? What if I really did plan this experience before I was born? What might I have been aiming to learn? What may be gained through the experience? How does this knowledge make me more loving, compassionate, and so on?

CONSIDER THESE THOUGHTS

1. You are here to be fully you. Be you, and no one else. I've found that the best way to become fully myself was to explore all the various aspects of me: personality, strengths, interests, astrology birth chart, numerology profile, thoughts/feelings, etc. Each of these brought clarity to the puzzle that is me. How about you? What does it mean to be you, in all your frailty and glory?
2. In many ways, life is a journey from the head to the heart. We plan life challenges to facilitate this journey to our hearts, so we may better know and love ourselves and others.
3. How have your parents, siblings, ethnicity, gender, socio-economic status, homes, schools, friends, and relationships contributed to opening your heart?

4. Some believe that déjà vu experiences are memories of pre-birth plans that show us we're in the right place.

5. Life plans seem to be set up so we experience who we are *not*, before we remember who we really are. Both sides are important.

6. Our plans contain "learning through opposites". It is the absence of something that best teaches us its value and meaning. Wanting to learn about compassion or forgiveness, one may choose to incarnate into a dysfunctional home.

7. From the higher perspective of the soul, the pain inherent in this learning process is temporary and brief, yet the resultant wisdom is literally eternal.

8. Since we have scripted the roles we play, we are not victims. No one is to blame. In fact, there is no blame. We all agreed to this challenge in the first place. (This worldview is not an excuse to go ahead and abuse others. It is an invitation to love yourself and others.)

9. When you can kiss adversity on the nose and welcome it as an invited guest, your suffering will be greatly reduced, and your heart will open wide.

10. You judge yourself, and you are the only one to do so. To release judgment and love with indiscriminant compassion is to remember who you really are.

11. We love the souls with whom we plan our lives. All of them, even those who play the role of enemy.

12. Those who love us are with us always, whether or not they incarnate alongside us. Heart connections are eternal.

13. Gratitude is an alignment of oneself with the frequency of Love Itself. Gratitude does not mean that we are *glad* we suffered. It means recognizing how the challenge fostered new growth and wisdom in us.
14. Confused actions are not failure. It is part of our development plan. We participate in these experiences to teach, and learn from, each other. When this growth is accomplished, the challenge faced has served its divine purpose.

When we return to spirit, or see now from a higher perspective, and recall the pre-birth plans we made with those who "wronged" us, their light and innocence becomes apparent to us once again. Until then, our challenge is to see their light while we are in body, beyond the veil of forgetfulness. We can do so by realizing that the people in our lives are eternal, nonphysical souls playing temporary roles on a physical stage. Each person we encounter is a spark of Divine Light, a loving, transcendent being with whom we are one.

> *"Before enlightenment chop wood, carry water.*
> *After enlightenment chop wood, carry water."*
> ~ Zen Proverb

SECTION 3

LIVING LOVED

OKAY, YOU'VE MADE it this far. If you've read the whole way through this book, you may have already opened your world-view to some peace inducing ideas. I invite you through to the finish. Or, you may have skipped to the end to read the punch line and missed out on rich resources for opening your heart and mind to fully embracing living loved. I invite you to go back and expand your worldview. You'll be glad you did.

WHAT DOES IT MEAN TO LIVE LOVED?

First, you might be asking, "What kind of love is she talking about?" Whole books have been written on the many different kinds of love, so let me be concise and specific here. The love I'm talking about is love with a capital L. This love is total, absolute, completely unconditional, all encompassing, and eternal. It's the spiritual kind of love you can trust that no matter what happens (ever), no matter what you do (or don't do), **you are adored**. Period. You don't have to do anything to earn this kind of love. This love is yours. It has your best interest at heart. It is watching over you and offering support and help and hope at all times. This Love is very kind, affectionate, and understanding of life's challenges.

To be clear, I'm not talking about romantic love that comes and goes, or obsessive love that is based on desperate need and confusion. Only the unconditional and unwavering love of our eternal Mother/Father will do.

If you've ever held your newborn child, or even baby puppies and kittens, and allowed the waves of love to wash over and through you, then you begin to have an idea of the joyous, tender, compassionate love I'm inviting you to feel. If you in your frail humanity can experience that depth of love, I wonder if you can magnify it by infinity and embrace the idea that Love Itself feels that way for you! There is an initial time of bonding that seats this love deeply into your soul, so I invite you to see yourself as an innocent infant and spend quality time connecting with that love, using your imagination, being held close, safe, and adored by Love Itself. Hypnotherapy is a great resource for bonding with Love Itself.

It would be easy to think that you would need to know something more, or do something special, to earn that big kind of love. From my experience, **the only way to get that love is to choose it, to step into it, and to receive it as a precious gift.** Indeed, it's already yours. Maybe you've forgotten, and are working on remembering that this love is an integral part of you, that you are already one with Love Itself. If you haven't already, be sure to read all the above sections for this book is full of thoughts that will help you remember who you are and remind you how to live loved.

When you live from fear, your thoughts, words, and actions are infused with anxiety, negative judgments, and confusion.

Fear places a screen before your eyes and ears, so that everything you experience is filtered and interpreted through that fear. You see the world and everything in it, not as they are, but distorted by that fear filter. However, since you can't "see" the filter, you are certain that your interpretations are correct. Pain and suffering are the clue that your filter is foggy.

Living loved is the opposite. You see the world through the filter-free eyes of love and respond in a whole new way. Living loved means that you think, speak, and act from the place of joyous freedom and love, for you know you are loved and safe. You connect frequently with Love Itself and allow it to flow through you. You choose to know that everything that comes your way comes through love first and is used by love to help you on your journey. Love says that all is well no matter what circumstances look like at the moment. Love encourages you to live fully present and peaceful, without story, where all help and inspiration is provided.

Love Itself sings a song to me that only I can hear.
~ Marie Maguire

LIVING LOVED IS A CHOICE
"Everything is God; God is love, so love is everything." Some version of this worldview is said by many spiritual teachers and traditions. Think about it, and breathe it into your bones. What is life like when you live as if every single thing, every

experience, every illness, and every challenge is Love, comes from Love, and leads you back to Love Itself? You could respond with, "Yes, but not when I have cancer. Yes, but not when my child dies young. Yes, but not when my marriage falls apart." (Remember that the 'but' cancels out the 'yes.') Nope, no exceptions! It doesn't work when you allow exceptions. Health/illness, marriage/divorce, gaining/losing, and yes, even death/birth all are God, and God is Love Itself so everything is love.

Or, you could, and many often do, live as if everything is to be feared, and even God is fearful because you may take the wrong path. In this chosen worldview there's little help or hope, and life is full of dread. You have to be on constant lookout to either run, or grab up what is needed for continued existence. Wow, that feels terrible even writing those words. I remember living in that fear-based worldview. *Cancel/clear!*

So, whether you live from love or fear, it's always a choice. Every single day, you get to choose, which way you wish to live. And, until you really feel and know yourself as loved, I invite you to act "as if" it was true! As if, everything that comes your way is love, and leads you to more love. "I am loved and I am safe!" is a great worldview to embrace.

What will your life be like as you choose to experience everything through love? How will things be different? What joys are to be found? What new adventures will be possible?

"You...were created to be loved.
So for you to live as if you were unloved is a limitation,
not the other way around...
Living unloved is like clipping a bird's wing
and removing its ability to fly... Love is
NOT the limitation; love is the flying.
I AM love."
~ Wm. Paul Young

BENEFITS OF LIVING LOVED

Who doesn't want to know that the journey is worth it? You may find it helpful to keep the following benefits out in front of you to encourage you along the way. They may even help you discover areas where you need healing and loving support.

- Loneliness dissolves and you're enveloped with a feeling of connection with All That Is.
- Gibberish in your brain settles down and you have a peaceful and quiet mind.
- You have less anxiety, stress, illness, and depression. You have a happier and healthier life.
- Suffering is an option that you are free to release or explore as you wish.
- Joy in living each moment with laughter in your heart center.

- Open and welcoming aspects of a higher vibration fill you.
- Draw ever more positive events and people your way.
- Awareness of deep innocence in yourself and others.
- Gratitude for each and every person and event in your life.
- Live in this moment, and allow everything to flow as it will.
- Have fun and relax into the flow of life.

"Love recognizes no barriers.
It jumps hurdles, leaps fences, penetrates walls
to arrive at its destination full of hope."
~ Maya Angelou

EXAMPLES OF LIVING LOVED

Example: You are on an airplane where a thought of possible disaster threatens your peace of mind. Your heart reminds you that you're deeply loved, and that when it's your time to die you will be guided and cared for through the process. You fall asleep knowing you're safe within Love Itself, and all is well.

Example: While working in a job that is stressful, the pressure is building to leave. You pray that you finish learning all you came to learn, and trust that you'll be inspired to leave when it is time. You relax and enjoy the process. Months later, at just the right moment, you get the job of which you've been dreaming.

Example: For whatever reason, you've run out of funds, and are facing homelessness. Since you know you're loved, and that everything comes through love before it gets to you, you can also know that this challenge comes from Love Itself. It's an opportunity to hold tight to what you know in your heart, to let go of what no longer serves you, and to trust that no matter what happens, all is well. Persistently ignoring fear, you stay curious and open, and follow inspiration that comes through love.

Example: People important to you have shut you out of their life. You do inner work (shadow/inquiry), so that you keep your heart open, loving, and kind. You choose to trust that all is as it needs to be at this time, and it will change when and as it is meant to change. Your focus turns to helping and loving others, knowing that you're deeply loved and adored by the Beloved.

Example: A conversation leads to your feeling offended. Because you now know that everything is about you, you do your inner work and question the stories in your head. You discover the belief that is causing your suffering and search until you find the real and loving truth behind it all. You give yourself what is needed, and only then have a loving and non-violent conversation with the friend who inspired this healing opportunity. The two of you grow closer and more connected as a result.

Example: You seem to be in a time of transition and no inspiration for action is forthcoming. You may be feeling squeezed on every side, yet you choose to remember that you're loved and safe within Love Itself. You've never been lost or late, and you trust Love to inspire you to take action at the right moment. You don't listen to the fear-based advice of well-meaning friends. You know in your bones that all is well even though you can't "see" it at this moment. You're developing the spiritual muscles that know peace within chaos.

Example: Wherever you are on the journey, the right books, songs, movies, conversations, etc. come along to speak love and peace into your soul. It is common for you to jump up in the middle of something to find your journal and write down the words of support coming from spirit. You keep those words in front of your mind to guide you on your way. Love knows where you're going better than you do!

Example: The world around you seems to be getting more violent and less respectful. You have a choice to live from fear or love. You choose love again and again, every single day. You allow love to be the touchstone for all thoughts, words, and actions, and trust love to keep you safe. No matter what challenges come your way you know they came through Love first and have your best and highest intentions in mind. You find loving, empowered, respectful responses to the violence and disrespect. Whether you live or die you are safe within Love Itself.

"All shall be well, all shall be well,
and all manner of things shall be well."
~ Julian of Norwich

"I am Yours. You are mine. We are one. All is well!"
~ Tosha Silver

THINGS TO TELL YOURSELF

Here are declarations to keep you moving forward. Use the one(s) that inspire you and say them again and again. Be persistent about finding your way home to Love Itself.

1. I now make my home in Love Itself.
2. My value and worth come from the only unshakable source, Love Itself.
3. I trust that everything that comes my way comes through love first.
4. All things work together for my good even if I can't see it in that moment.
5. I'm grateful for everything and everyone, for they are my teachers.
6. I focus my mind on life-giving sayings such as: I'm loved and I know it!
7. I participated in the planning of this life and I choose to grow and learn as I go.

8. I live in this moment, and move forward when inspired by love.
9. I'm open to following my curiosity and zeal, trusting that love guides me.
10. No inspiration equals no action taken. Stillness can be an act of faith.
11. Love inspires my words and actions towards myself and others.
12. All transitions are guided. I'm safe always, even when passing from life to life.

"I wish I could show you when you are lonely,
or in darkness,
the astonishing light of your being."
~ Hafiz

SUMMARY

Now what? You've read all or parts of this book, and may feel a multitude of emotions. Thoughts may be in a jumble, and your worldview on the edge of collapse. Don't listen to fearful friends. Please seek loving guidance and follow Love Itself.

Or you may feel tremendous relief that you've found words that validate your own spiritual experience. You now know that you're not alone on the journey. Keep growing and find spiritual compatriots, deep soul friends, to share in the journey.

Or you may think you already know this stuff, and wonder why you're still suffering. You may know it, yet if you're still suffering then you don't believe it. Read this book repeatedly until you let the information flow down out of your head and into your heart, where it inspires new action. Guidance with this transformative process is always a good idea.

Wherever you are in the above continuum, keep choosing love over and over and over again, until you believe it and then feel it, and then you allow love to transform every aspect of your life. Living loved is a choice every moment, until it becomes your first nature.

I INVITE YOU TO REMEMBER

1. Review the thoughts over and over again until you know them in your heart and bones, not only in your head.
2. You are loved, through and through!
3. You are safe within Love Itself.
4. Living loved is sometimes a moment by moment choice.
5. Love will lead you safely forward and toward good things. There is no rush.
6. Choose your thoughts carefully. They create your experience in this life.

7. Breathe in the thoughts and emotions, and let your heart expand to hold you safely.
8. Take no actions inspired by fear. Ever. Be still until love moves you.
9. Speak no words inspired by fear. Ever. Be silent until love speaks through you.
10. Don't listen to the fearful. Love them certainly, but go the way love leads you instead.
11. Embrace ideas you are ready for. Keep what brings love and peace to you.
12. When you are ready for a new idea, which is the perfect moment and not a moment sooner, embrace that idea, and knit it into your heart.
13. Let go of certainty for yourself and others. "I don't know," is great wisdom.
14. Remain open and follow your curiosity, trusting love to lead you safely.
15. Let others journey in ways that make sense to them. Trust Love Itself to lead them safely.
16. Spirituality that leads to Love Itself will also invite you to cry, laugh, create, and play.
17. Be on the lookout for spiritual companions who are inspired to be by your side for awhile, arm in arm, each of you delighting in the other's journey.
18. Remember that love likes to work backwards and forwards through all time, space, and dimensions, to bring healing to every part of your body and soul. Embrace love with every aspect of your being.

ACTION STEPS

When making changes to your worldview, it may be most comfortable to start small. Maybe embrace only one new worldview at a time. Choose one idea and delve into it through your personal style of research. Read books on the topic, find a spiritual journey coach, write in your journal, watch YouTube videos, meditate, create a list of thoughts to focus on, lead or join a discussion group, and be very patient and loving toward yourself. Ask for help from Love Itself, and be on the lookout for all the ways Love supports you on your journey to living loved.

> *Sweet Love at the center of all ~*
> *I breathe Love in and am transformed.*
> ~ Marie Maguire

WHAT MATTERS MOST?

In the beginning, middle, and the end: Love is all that matters and love is all there is. Let us remember to love ourselves first, so that from that state of fullness we may also love God and our neighbor.

> *"What a different relationship begins to develop*
> *when you realize*
> *that God is head-over-heels in love with you.*
> *God is simply giddy about you. He*
> *just can't help loving you.*

*And he loves you deeply, recklessly
and extravagantly-just as you are."*
~ David Benner

*"The world is what you believe it to be
And it changes as you change."*
~ Byron Katie

IN THE END
I don't need to be right, and I don't need to make you wrong. I may even be mistaken about some or most of this book, and I'm okay with that possibility, for I know that I'm loved. I'm not interested in arguing about these ideas, for quarrelling comes from fear and produces only more fear and separation. Your path is right for you, and my path is perfectly awesome for me. **Let us each follow our own creative path to Love Itself.** And allow everyone else to do the same.

Beloved, let us open to living loved, and let us love one another, for we are part of Love Itself.

*"...no one else can possibly know
the unique contours of (your) own true-path.
Since you are the only one living in your temple,
only you can know its scriptures
and interpretive structure.*

*The next step is right there inside you,
divinely imprinted on the souls of your feet."*
~ Jeff Brown

EPILOGUE

It may be interesting for you to know that, almost as soon as I finished writing this book, my client load dissolved, all efforts to produce income were unsuccessful, rent went unpaid, and I evicted myself from the home I was renting. I tried and couldn't sell my possessions, so I ended up giving most of them away. Then my computer died. Money has been a prominent teacher for me in this life, and here was the perfect set up and another opportunity to see if I really believed what I wrote in this book. Certainly, this new challenge was one more opportunity to choose between fear and love.

Alas, it is time to publish the book and this story is still unfolding. I've no clue what comes next. I'm certain that all is well and all shall be well. Perhaps I'll have the opportunity to meet you at an event and share more of my adventures in living loved. Blessed be the journey.

RESOURCES

DISCUSSION GUIDE

DISCUSSION LEADER GUIDELINES

1. As the group leader, it's vital that you set the expectations and maintain the safety standards. You declare what's acceptable and what isn't, so be firm and loving in your leadership.
2. Good discussion questions are open-ended, lead to curiosity, inspire a variety of responses, and encourage members to dialogue with each other respectfully.
3. They depend on a careful reading of the text and asking people to share their experience.
4. Invite participants to imagine and then share what their life will be like when they incorporate new ideas into their life.
5. Please, don't use the word "Why?" This question too often leads to defensiveness and argument.
6. Instead, use: how, when, what, and where to draw out further discussion.
   a. How will you know?
   b. What does that look like?
   c. What if it's true that you're loved through and through?

d. What would you do if you weren't afraid?

e. I'm curious if you've _____?

f. I wonder if you're feeling _____?

g. What will you do when _____?

h. How will you feel when _____ is no longer an issue?

i. If not now, when? In what ways will it be better/easier then?

j. What I hear you saying is that you believe _____. Is that true?

k. How do you know _____? How specifically?

l. According to whom? Who says _____?

m. I'm hearing/feeling suffering in your words. Is that true?

n. What might it look/feel like when love infuses that situation? (open, expansive, safe...)

o. If you did know, what would the answer be?

p. What's important to you about that idea?

q. How does that _____ fit into your current worldview?

r. In what way does it benefit you to keep that idea in your worldview?

s. How will things be different when you let it go?

t. What else is possible?

7. If you find people dropping out of the group, you may wish to discover the reasons. Did they feel "other-ized,"** unsafe, or judged? Even if they refuse to return, this issue needs to be handled for the group to thrive and for individuals to be healthfully supported within Love Itself.

DISCUSSION HOUSEKEEPING

To ensure that this discussion group is a safe and loving place, we will be following these guidelines:

1. All ideas and feelings will be listened to with respect. Be kind, courteous and loving.
2. Each person will be given equal opportunities to partici-pate. No one person may dominate the discussion. Let us leave moments of silence, so that the more introverted among us feel free to participate.
3. Verbal violence is not allowed.
   a. You may wish to review the section on nonviolent communication and then continue offering sugges-tions for keeping the conversation safe.
   b. Empower each person to reveal when they feel judged, unsafe or "otherized."**
   c. Allow each person to have his/her own unique spiri-tual journey – without judgment.
4. You may listen, discuss, and ask questions for clarity; you may not debate, interrupt, preach, argue, offer advice, nor raise your voice. Ask yourself, "Are my words loving, kind and merciful?"
5. You may be asked to leave if you're unable to speak with love and allow others to feel safe.
   a. Private warning – using loving and nonviolent words
   b. Public warning – using loving and nonviolent words
   c. Removal from the group – with regret and open hearts

**Otherized – means being made to feel different in an unacceptable way: wrong personality, wrong gender or race, wrong worldview, wrong clothing style, and so on to infinity.

"(Advice giving) is a strategy for abandoning each other, while appearing to be concerned."
~ Parker Palmer

SUGGESTED QUESTIONS/DISCUSSIONS (NO PARTICULAR ORDER)

1. Select any of the numbered topics. Read the section aloud, discuss the topic, discover how life will be different with the new worldview, and explore how to embrace the new idea.

   For instance:
   • Talk about nonviolence and practice several real or imagined scenarios within the group.
   • Discuss either/or thinking and how it feels to limit possibilities.
   • Explore AND - and how it is experienced in conversation.
2. Tell us about your spiritual mentors and their impact on your life.
3. If you wish, please tell us about your spiritual journey.
4. How have your views of yourself or your parents influenced how you experience God (or religion)?
5. What areas in your life have been healed, so that you now see more clearly?

6. What things happened in your life to cause you to be certain there is a God who is both infinite and personally caring?

7. If you did choose to experience this (life challenge), how might you have planned to benefit? Answer from the wisest and most loving part of yourself. And now, from your higher self.

8. What might a beloved spiritual teacher have to say to you about _____?

9. What do you consider to be two major turning points in your life?

10. What are two or three personal truths upon which you base your decision-making?

11. Let's share some decisions we've experienced that were based in fear or based in love. How do you experience and describe the difference?

12. After reading this book, how do you now view heartache / challenges / relationships?

13. What spiritual texts bless your spiritual journey? Share a favorite passage or two.

14. What is your experience of Jesus / Buddha / Mohammed, etc. (not the religions) and their messages of love and forgiveness?

15. What religious structures / traditions do you enjoy and thrive within?

16. In what ways do you see your worldview expanding? How do you know? What evidence do you see?

17. What are your joys, passions, curiosities? What do they lead you to explore?

18. How do you take ideas out of your head and incorporate them into your living experience?
19. Tell us how your life is opening and expanding because of these ideas.
20. What support do you need to feel safe to search, to question, and to explore Love Itself?
21. What might change in your life and relationships as you continue this worldview expansion?
22. If your higher self were to give you support or guidance, what would it say?
23. How may we support you?

"Truth evolves within us, between us and around us,
as we participate in the eternal conversation."
~ Parker Palmer

RECOMMENDED READING

- *Autobiography of a Yogi* by Paramahansa Yogananda
- *Big Magic* by Elizabeth Gilbert
- *Buddhist Boot Camp* by Timber Hawkeye
- *Cosmic Cradle* by Elizabeth Carman and Neil Carman
- *Creating an Extraordinary Relationship* by Paul Zohav, M.Ed.
- *Dark Night of the Soul* and *St. John of the Cross* by Mirabai Starr
- *Falling into Grace* by Adyashanti

- *Finding Your Way in a Wild New World* by Martha Beck
- *For Love of the Real: A Story of Life's Mystical Secret* by Llewellyn Vaughan-Lee
- *Hidden Wholeness* by Parker Palmer
- *Love Warrior* by Glennon Doyle Melton
- *Loving What Is* by Byron Katie
- *Magic Past Lives* by Atasha Fyfe
- *Never Alone* and *Joshua* by Father Joseph E Girzone
- *Nonviolent Communication: A Language of Life* by Marshall Rosenberg, PhD
- *Past Lives, Present Miracles* by Denise Linn
- *The Afterlife of Billie Fingers* by Annie Kagan
- *The Dark Night of the Soul* by Gerald May, MD
- *The Dark Side of the Light Chasers* by Debbie Ford
- *The Gentle Way* by Tom T. Moore
- *The Gift of Fear*, by Gavin DeBecker
- *The Shack: Where Tragedy Confronts Eternity* by Wm. Paul Young
- *The Untethered Soul* by Michael Singer
- *The Velveteen Rabbit* by Margery Williams
- *Visionary Activist Astrology* by Caroline W. Casey
- *What the Mystics Know — Seven Pathways to your Deeper Self* by Richard Rohr
- *Who Ordered this Truckload of Dung?* by Ajahn Brahm
- *Why Not be a Mystic* by Frank X. Tuoti
- *Women Who Run with the Wolves* by Clarissa Pinkola Estés

For fun, here are some of my favorite fiction writers:
CS Lewis, JRR Tolkien, Agatha Christie, JK Rowling, John

Stephens, Mercedes Lackey, Neil Gaiman, Jane Austin, James Herriot, Raymond Feist, Shel Silverstein, and Dr. Seuss.

Many of these titles and/or authors have been referenced or quoted in this book. They are among my greatest teachers and I highly recommend each and every one of them. They are great resources to enhance your own continued journey to a wider worldview. I invite you to let your curiosity and zeal lead you to the books, authors, and ideas that are right for you! With Love as your guidepost, you will always find your way home to living loved.

If you are one of the beloved quoted authors and, for whatever reason, would like your words removed from the next edition, please contact me to express your wishes. Thank you for helping me on my journey from fear to love!

The following poem has run in the silent background of my life and helped me more than I may ever know.

Don't Quit (a poem)

When things go wrong, as they sometimes will,
When the road you're trudging seems all uphill,
When the funds are low and the debts are high,
And you want to smile, but you have to sigh,

When care is pressing you down a bit,
Rest, if you must, but don't you quit.
Life is queer with its twists and turns,
As every one of us sometimes learns,
And many a failure turns about,
When he might have won had he stuck it out;
Don't give up though the pace seems slow -
You may succeed with another blow.
Often the goal is nearer than,
It seems to a faint and faltering man,
Often the struggler has given up,
When he might have captured the victor's cup,
And he learned too late when the night slipped down,
How close he was to the golden crown.
Success is failure turned inside out -
The silver tint of the clouds of doubt,
And you never can tell how close you are,
It may be near when it seems so far,
So stick to the fight when you're hardest hit -
It's when things seem worst that you must not quit.
~ John Greenleaf Whittier

"If you say only one prayer in a day,
make it, "Thank you!"
~Rumi

SECTION 5

CLOSING

CLIENT TESTIMONIALS

I HAD SUCH a wonderful time in each of my sessions. Your influence on my life has helped me feel more conscious and at peace with my consciousness. My mind now releases its grip on identification with struggle and realigns with its understanding of the nature of peaceful coexistence with all the other flurries and furies of the world. A quiet mind is a more productive mind. Thank you! ~ **M**

Marie is truly remarkable at what she does. It is clear that she has an innate and special talent for understanding the underlying root causes of issues, allowing her to help clients address challenges much more quickly than applying a classical level of cognitive therapy. Marie's professionalism, kindness, and compassion are beyond reproach. It is clear that helping people to realize their goals is her true passion.

Marie possesses a wonderful ability to craft sessions specific for your needs by asking pertinent questions and then designing relaxing healing processes around this. In the six sessions that I had, in which I was an active participant, I was able to realize significant changes in my thinking and how I framed problems. I very highly recommend working with Marie to help you "unravel" problems to get to the root of challenges to attain a greater level of self-analysis and acceptance that will allow you to lead a more liberating and peaceful life. ~ L

Before my first session with Marie, I had received hypno-therapy sessions from two other practitioners and had heard several self-hypnosis audios. After that first session, I knew I would never go to anyone else again. Before we started, Marie took the time to really get to know me and what my needs were. I had been mulling over the idea of having chil-dren, and coming to terms with whether I would make a good mother. During the session, I felt at ease, relaxed, and aware of everything that was being said. It was amazing to me how much insight I learned about myself in such a short amount of time. What was even more incredible was how subtle the work was. For days afterward, I noticed change in my behavior around the issues that had been addressed. It really hit home during a conversation with my husband, and in my mind I said, "Well, of course we're going to have children!" It wasn't something that I had ever confidently thought before. I felt an assurance that was unexpected, and I couldn't wait for my next session with Marie. ~ C

I came to Marie as I was trying to decide whether to work on my 14-year marriage or move on. Marie was the sixth in a long line of therapists, and I wanted to try hypnother-apy, as I'm prone to a 'you can't tell me what to do' atti-tude that hinders traditional therapy. When Marie opened the door and smiled, I instantly relaxed and felt at ease and comfortable. Marie has a quiet and calm way about her that allows one to be honest with oneself and know there is no judgment. To address my marriage, I decided to try past life regression. Learning about my past life with my present husband made me understand that though we have our issues, we asked to be together; that our time together is precious, and the challenges we face every day are the bargain we made to be together this time around. I'm so happy I found Marie! ~ **W**

I was having trouble managing the anger I feel over life's unfairness, and one of the many tools Marie taught me was how to embrace the anger, not talk it away, and to grow it and explode it. I loved that! There was no one telling me not to feel a certain way, or making me talk about why I felt a certain way, but to embrace that intense feeling and blow it up. It was very liberating to allow myself to feel anger and know that I can control it without stuffing it away. After years of bottling up my anger, Marie taught me to work with that energy, control it, and let it flow through me rather than fighting it. I feel empowered to handle my own feelings. ~ **L**

I am a highly sensitive person who struggled with a lifetime of anxiety, low self-esteem, and depression. Working with Marie Maguire is better than any other counseling, personal growth and/or development work I've ever experienced. We touched the deep subconscious and healed the blind spots so I'm able to move forward quickly and easily. I now have access to who I really am! I'm peaceful, joyful, and fully present in my life every day! ~ **L**

My life gets way too busy and chaotic. After spending time with Marie, I am deeply grounded, my heart is peaceful, and I have my head on straight. Most of the time I have no idea what was said that made such a difference, but I know that I'm changed and feel renewed. Thank you Marie for coming into my life! ~ **C**

Dealing with a life-long depression motivated me to seek both conventional and non-conventional treatments. Years of pharmaceuticals helped, but the yo-yo effect of anti-depressant medications failing, and then searching for the new panacea, had left me disillusioned. After my first session with you, I knew I was on the right path. By using a gentle, trance-induced process, you helped me replace a life-altering memory to a non-invasive history page in my past. In another session, I was gently guided using energy management to release unhealthy relationship bonds. In addition, you've taught me to re-frame what I thought was depression to a new appreciation of my gifts as a Sensitive, and this is only after three sessions! I can't thank you enough or more highly recommend you to future clients. ~ **C**

What a difference a year makes! When I first went to see Marie I was in crisis. A year later, I am free of depression and anger. I work with Marie every month to keep myself on an even keel and to continue moving forward as I navigate this journey we call life. I highly recommend working with Marie. ~ **S**

ACKNOWLEDGMENTS

Heartfelt thanks goes to everyone who participated in my lifetime journey as Marie Maguire. In ways beyond measure, each and every one of you is part of this endeavor to put *Living Loved: a path to peace* into print.

Julie Calvez Stinson you are a hermit-angel-mystic, and a blessing in my life. I'm forever grateful for your deep soul friendship, and all you do to continue teaching me about love.

For the editing and proof reading suggestions, I'm indebted to Adair E., Elenjo Schaff, Ericka O'Cain, Jennifer Bancroft, Julie Stinson, and Kieara Brodhakker. Your ideas and proof reading skills vastly improved the outcome of this work. I take full responsibility for the remaining creative use of punctuation.

A special thank you goes to the many friends who've supported me along the way: Aaron, Alan, Artie, Carolyn, Colleen, Diane, Ericka, Erin, Heather, Ilze, Jason, Jenn, Jennifer, Jules, Kate, Kimba, Michelle N., Michelle and Ken, Pam, Rebecca, Sherry, Troy and Cindy, Wm, and Wayne and Deborah. I'm also deeply indebted to my friends Paul and Rita for providing a peaceful haven, which allowed me to prepare this book for publication. May the blessings each of you gave be multiplied back to you with joy.

For the opportunity to repeatedly practice putting these thoughts into sensible language, I'm deeply indebted to my clients. You've taught me so much. You've blessed and enriched me in my journey as a spiritual guide. May Love Itself continue to make your lives richer and more peaceful, as you continue moving toward the wholeness of living loved.

Blessed be each and every one of you, dear readers! Without knowing it you also have pulled me onward to share these words. Thank you!

⌒

FEEDBACK

Like our spiritual journeys, this book will continue growing and improving. If there's something you'd like to see added, any grammatical corrections, any insight for upcoming editions, or if this book comforts you and helps your journey in any way, I would love to hear from you! I'd also be delighted to hear about any attribution corrections. As one who has read a countless number of books, it is difficult to remember who said what, and to know when one of my thoughts is mine alone, or inspired directly from one of those great authors. If you find words that seem to be a direct quote from an unnamed author, I'd be delighted to hear about it so I may honor that author in the next edition. Also, I couldn't find attributions or copy write information for the Zen koans (teaching tales) I've shared in this edition. Feel free to enlighten me on their source.

GETTING CONNECTED:

Email: LivingLoved@Marie-Maguire.com.
I'll do my best to respond whenever feasible.
Facebook page: https://www.facebook.com/MarieMaguire777
Living Loved Facebook group: http://www.facebook.com/groups/LivingLoved77
Twitter: https://twitter.com/MarieMaguire77

Here, at the end, I've a favor to ask! If this book has been a positive experience, I'd be grateful if you'd post a review on Amazon.com. Your thoughts really do make a difference, and you may inspire others along the way. Thank you for your support!

> *"You know quite well, deep within you,*
> *that there is only a single magic,*
> *a single power, a single salvation*
> *and that is called loving."*
> ~ Hermann Hesse

About the Author

Marie Maguire in 30 Seconds

- I'm passionate about bringing peace to our world one mind at a time.
- I'm dedicated to helping people become freed from fear, and awaken to the beauty of living loved.
- I receive great pleasure in helping creative thinkers and feelers discover who they are, and guiding them as they blossom.
- I'm inspired by people who are brave enough to transform adversity into spiritual growth, and courageous enough to allow their hearts to be broken open.
- I live, love, and teach from a borderless spirituality.
- I write, paint, and enjoy nature most every day, because I can't help myself.
- I'm moved by laughter and fuzzy creatures, all forms of art, and awesome displays of nature.

Marie Maguire, MA, CHt

Spiritual Counselor, Clinical Hypnotherapist
NLP practitioner, Coach for Highly Sensitive People (HSPs)
Natal and Past Life Regression
BA Biblical Counseling

MA Christian Counseling Psychology
MA Editorial Design
600+ hours Clinical Hypnotherapy and NLP
INFJ / HSP / Mystic / Contemplative / Intuitive
A follower of Jesus, Buddha, and Yogananda...
"I seek balance in all things."

79720753R00173

Made in the USA
San Bernardino, CA
17 June 2018